SQL
THE STRUCTURED
QUERY LANGUAGE

Dr. Carolyn J. Hursch and
Dr. Jack L. Hursch

TAB Professional and Reference Books

Division of TAB BOOKS Inc.
Blue Ridge Summit, PA

ORACLE and SQL*Plus are registered trademarks of Oracle Corporation, Belmont, Calif.
IBM is the registered trademark of International Business Machines Corporation.

FIRST EDITION
FOURTH PRINTING

Printed in the United States of America

Library of Congress Cataloging in Publication Data

Hursch, Carolyn J.
SQL, the structured query language.

Bibliography: p.
Includes index.
1. SQL (Computer program language).   2. Data base
   management. I. Hursch, Jack L. II. Title.
QA76.73.S67H87   1988   005.75′65   87-33507
              ISBN 0-8306-9016-6
              ISBN 0-8306-3016-3 (pbk.)

TAB BOOKS Inc. offers software for
sale. For information and a catalog,
please contact TAB Software Department,
Blue Ridge Summit, PA 17294-0850.

Questions regarding the content of this book
should be addressed to:

Reader Inquiry Branch
TAB BOOKS Inc.
Blue Ridge Summit, PA 17294-0214

Contents

Introduction

THE ADVENT AND SUCCESSFUL IMPLEMENTATION OF RELATIONAL DATA-
bases has brought with it the need for a database language that
is user-friendly enough for the casual user, yet convenient enough
for the programmer and applications builder. The structured
query language now called SQL (pronounced "sequel"), after a rapid
period of evolution, is emerging to fill that need. The end user can
easily learn and understand SQL, and it can be embedded in procedural languages such as C, COBOL, or PL/I. It also provides a much-
needed common avenue of discourse between the end user and the
programmer. This fact alone provides inestimable benefits in smoothing
out the transition from paper files to computerized database systems.

This text sets forth the structure and syntax of SQL and discusses
the extent of its use in commercial systems now on the market.

Since our purpose is to present the complete picture of SQL,
its mathematical structure is traced from its basis in first-order logic
to its present-day role as a structured query language. This will
be of interest mainly to computer science professionals and system
developers. For that same audience, as well as for the end user who
is not a computer professional, all of the SQL features are exhibited
and worked through step by step with examples.

Exercises at the end of most chapters make the text appropriate
for classroom use.

The contents of the text are as follows: Chapter 1 traces the
history of the development of SQL from E. F. Codd's articles in

the early 1970s, which set forth the principles of a relational database, through the Chamberlin articles of the late 1970s, to the current proposal now before the American National Standards Institute (ANSI) for a standard SQL language. This chapter also defines the terms and the notation system used throughout the text.

Chapter 2 contains an overview of all of the components of the SQL language: the SQL commands, keywords, datatypes, and value expressions supported by SQL. The three main types of statements, data definition, data manipulation and data control, are listed, and the syntax for each is shown. The syntax for the various expressions, connectives, predicates, and functions that make up the SQL language are also presented.

Chapter 3 contains explanations and examples of the use of SQL table expressions and predicates in preparation for using them to set up a database in the next chapter.

Chapter 4 illustrates the use of the data definition statements CREATE, ALTER, and DROP, and gives examples of these statements as they are used to define and modify tables in an illustrative database system.

Chapter 5 illustrates the use of the data manipulation statements INSERT, UPDATE, and DELETE TABLE, and the query statement SELECT . . . FROM . . . WHERE. Since creating views (unlike creating tables) involves data manipulation, it is included in this chapter.

Chapter 6 explains the use of the data control statements and discusses the security and integrity constraints that may be invoked using SQL.

Chapter 7 shows the use of aggregate functions, logical operators, and subqueries as SQL employs them, and includes examples of the use of NOT with each of these.

Since joins are the basis of the efficient use of a relational database, Chapter 8 is devoted exclusively to this topic. Equijoins and non-equijoins are explained, as well as the Cartesian product, natural joins, and outer joins.

In Chapter 9, views are discussed in detail. With a well-designed database, the end user will be using views rather than base tables most of the time. At the same time, not all operations possible with tables are possible with views. Therefore, SQL operations on views are explained and the view-update problem is discussed.

Also, in Chapter 9, the use of indices is discussed, and the optimum formation of queries to speed up the retrieval process is outlined.

SQL has been said to resemble the tuple relational calculus; however, it contains properties taken from both the relational algebra and the relational calculus. Therefore, in Chapter 10 the elements of relational algebra are developed and related to SQL.

Chapter 11 develops the elements of the first-order logic needed for the tuple relational calculus as discussed by Codd [14]. Interpretations as developed in the propositional calculus and the predicate calculus with quantifiers are explained, and their extension in the predicate calculus to a database scheme is exhibited. This database scheme is then shown to be an interpretation determining a form of the predicate calculus known as the tuple relational calculus. The extension of the idea of an interpretation is shown to determine what is retrieved by means of a query formulated in the tuple relational calculus. Finally, the examples and exercises show how the tuple relational calculus queries are converted to SQL queries.

Thus, Chapter 11 demonstrates how SQL developed from the need for a query language, through first-order logic, to a user-friendly relational database interface.

Chapter 12 presents *embedded SQL*, a form of SQL that can be embedded in computer programs and be converted to the host language code with a precompiler. *Cursors* (implementor-defined work areas for holding relational tables obtained from queries) are discussed, as well as the embedded SQL commands for manipulating cursors. The goal in Chapter 12 is to present embedded SQL as it now exists under the current ANSI standard and most current implementations, without limiting the presentation to any one implementation. Suggestions are made for modifying the embedding process to make the programmer's task less onerous and produce bug-free programs. These suggestions are demonstrated by examples of SQL embedded in short C language modules that the programmer can modify to fit his own implementation and requirements.

Chapter 13 describes the use of SQL in the principal commercial databases now on the market.

Also in Chapter 13, the new as well as the potential uses of SQL in connection with knowledge bases are discussed. Expert systems are taking on more complex problems requiring larger knowledge bases. There is also commercial interest in expert systems that will run on low-cost hardware. These developments lead naturally into the use of database management techniques for knowledge bases. SQL is beginning to play a part in this process as a language that can be used by an expert system to submit queries to the knowledge base.

A bibliography provides the interested reader with sources of further information on all of the topics covered.

1

How SQL Got Here

THE FOLLOWING IS A BRIEF HISTORY OF THE DEVELOPMENT OF THE SQL data sublanguage. The latter part of this chapter is devoted to the notation and definitions used in the text.

1.1 Development of SQL

When E. F. Codd introduced the concept of a relational database [14] in 1970, he suggested that "the adoption of a relational model of data . . . permits the development of a universal data sublanguage based on an applied predicate calculus." Although he indicated the requirements and the advantages of such a language, he did not attempt at that time to devise one. In a later article [17], he discussed the concept of *relational completeness* (a term that he coined and that is now widely used) of a database sublanguage.

Acceptance of the relational idea was relatively slow (but slow only in comparison with the usual speed of technical advances in the computer field). Therefore, it was not until 1974 that Chamberlin and Boyce [8] published an article suggesting the form of a structured query language, which at that time was called SEQUEL. The following year, Boyce, Chamberlin, King, and Hammer [7] published an article setting forth the sublanguage SQUARE which was much like SEQUEL except that SQUARE used mathematical expressions rather than the English terms of SEQUEL. Both languages are shown by the authors to be relationally complete in the sense outlined by Codd in his 1970 and 1971 articles *[14,17]*. "Relationally complete" in that context means "at least as powerful as the tuple relational calculus."

The SQUARE article was followed by another article by Chamberlin and others in 1976 *[10]* when the name was changed to SEQUEL 2, and it was used as the query language for the IBM research database *System R*.

By the time Chamberlin wrote in 1980, *[11]* summarizing user-experience with the language, the name had been changed to its present form: SQL, denoting a *Structured Query Language*. A test of SQL by a broad group of users resulted in several additions to the language, including the addition of *outer joins* to SQL's capabilities, which Codd had already suggested in his 1979 article *[21]*.

Further development reported in other articles *[2,3,6,9,12]* resulted in present-day SQL.

During the last decade, relational databases have emerged and become more popular than the hierarchical and network databases that preceded them. This trend appears to be accelerating. To inject some order into the rapidly increasing literature on relational databases, Codd in 1985 *[19,20]* laid down twelve principles, at least six of which must be satisfied in order for a database to call itself *fully relational*. These were preceded by one overall general rule, called "Rule Zero," which reads as follows:

Rule 0. Relational database management. For any system that is advertised as, or claimed to be, a relational database management system, that system must be able to manage databases entirely through its relational capabilities.

The 12 specific rules follow.

1. **Representation of information.** All information in a relational database is represented explicitly at the logical level and in exactly one way—by values in tables.
2. **Guaranteed logical accessibility.** Each and every datum (atomic value) in a relational database is guaranteed to be logically accessible by resorting to a combination of table name, primary key value, and column name.
3. **Systematic representation of missing information.** Null values (distinct from the empty character string or a string of blank characters and distinct from zero or any other number)

are supported in fully relational database management systems for representing missing information and inapplicable information in a systematic way independent of data type.

4. **Dynamic online catalog.** The database description is represented at the local level in the same way as ordinary data, so that authorized users can apply the same relational language to its interrogation as they apply to the regular data.

5. **Comprehensive data sublanguage.** A relational system may support several languages and various modes of terminal use (for example, the "fill in the blanks" mode). There must be, however, at least one language whose statements are expressible, per some well-defined syntax, as character strings, and that is comprehensive in supporting all of the following items:

Data definition
View definition
Data manipulation (interactive and by program)
Integrity constraints
Authorization
Transaction boundaries (begin, commit, and rollback)

6. **Updatable views.** All views that are theoretically updatable are also updatable by the system.

7. **High-level insert, update and delete.** The capability of handling a base relation or a derived relation as a single operand applies not only to the retrieval of data, but also to the insertion, update, and deletion of data.

8. **Physical data independence.** Application programs and terminal activities remain logically unimpaired whenever any changes are made in either storage representations or access methods.

9. **Logical data independence.** Application programs and terminal activities remain logically unimpaired when information-preserving changes of any kind that theoretically permit unimpairment are made to the base tables.

10. **Integrity independence.** Integrity constraints specific to a particular database must be definable in the relational data sublanguage and storable in the catalog, not in the application program.

11. **Distribution independence.** Whether or not a system supports database distribution, it must have a data sublanguage that

can support distributed databases without impairing application programs or terminal activities.

12. **The nonsubversion rule.** If a relational system has a low-level (single-record-at-a-time) language, that low-level cannot be used to subvert or bypass the integrity rules and constraints expressed in the higher level relational language (multiple-records-at-a-time).

A proof that SQL is relationally complete has been outlined by Date *[26]*. Chapter 11 of this book presents a discussion of the tuple relational calculus beginning with classical logic, and in this development we demonstrate the conversion of logic queries to SQL.

The fact that the developers knew ahead of time what SQL should be and what it would be required to do gave it a strong theoretical foundation. This is probably a first in computer language development because most computer languages in use today are the result of a basic idea supplemented by a great deal of *ad hoc* patching to meet problems as they arise. This fact—specifying the need for SQL before developing of the mechanics of it—gave rise to an elegantly parsimonious language consisting of relatively few commands that can be used to satisfy most of the needs of a very complex database. Its simplicity makes SQL convenient for the casual user as well as the sophisticated developer. It can be used for *ad hoc* queries, and it can also be embedded in a host-language program.

At this time, there are several structured languages in existence that are being used for querying relational databases. However, SQL appears to be the one most widely adopted for commercial use.

The American National Standards Institute (ANSI) has now published a standard[1] setting forth the syntax and semantics for SQL, called *Database Language SQL [1]*. The ANSI Standard uses the *Backus-Naur Form* (BNF) of syntactic notation, which, for the reader's convenience, is not used here. See reference *[50]*. Additional standards for the SQL language are planned by ANSI; topics now under consideration to be published as addenda to the existing standard are referential integrity, enhanced transaction management, specification of certain user-defined rules, enhanced character-handling facilities, and support for national character sets.

Over the years, changes have been made in SQL as a result of product testing, user input, and further development. This book

---

1. The publication containing the present SQL standard (ANSI X3.136-1986) and any subsequent additions to that standard can be obtained from the American National Standards Institute, Inc. 1430 Broadway, New York, NY 110018.

will attempt to incorporate all such changes that have appeared in the literature, even though they may not appear in the ANSI standard. It also includes the complete IBM version of SQL *[35,36,37]*.

1.2 Notation

The following notation will be used throughout this book:

1. All SQL commands will be written in capital letters, for example: CREATE TABLE.
2. Words that are to be filled in from the user's own installation or from the fictitious database used as an example, will be written in lowercase italics, as in *tablename*. Thus, the term:

   CREATE TABLE *tablename*

   indicates that the SQL Command CREATE TABLE is to be followed by a table name chosen by the user.
3. An asterisk (*) will be used to indicate "all columns fitting the description," as in:

   SELECT   *
   FROM   *tablename*
   WHERE   City = ' Dallas';

   which is interpreted as: "SELECT all columns FROM the named table WHERE the value in the City column is "Dallas."
       The single quotes appear around the word "Dallas" in the above WHERE clause because Dallas is a column value, i.e., a datum. Any character string that is a column value must be surrounded by single quotes.
4. Ellipses will be used to indicate the continuation of a series, such as

   column1, column2, . . . , columnN.

   which is interpreted as: "column 1, column 2, and any other numbered columns, in order, to the end of the list of columns."
5. So that the host language will interpret them as a single character string, two or more adjacent words will be connected by an underline whenever they are to be displayed as a

table or column heading (filled in by the user) as in:

employee__name

6. Every SQL statement should be ended with an implementor-defined termination symbol. In this text we will indicate the end of a SQL statement with a semicolon (;).
7. The desired list of columns in a query (i.e., that list of columns appearing after the SELECT command) will be called the *target list*. This is in keeping with Codd's usage of that term in the tuple relational calculus.
8. Optional inclusions in a SQL statement will be indicated by placing them within [brackets]. For example,

CREATE VIEW *viewname* [*column__names*]

means that the inclusion of column names in the CREATE VIEW statement shown is optional.

1.3 Definitions

In keeping with the fact that SQL is an adjunct to a relational database management system, the following terms are defined within the relational context:

In 1971 Codd [18] introduced the idea of using "tables" as the main database structure. He describes a table as a rectangular array with the following properties:

P_1: It is column-homogeneous; in other words, in any selected column the items are all of the same kind, whereas items in different columns need not be of the same kind.

P_2: Each item is a simple number or a character string (thus, for example, if we look at the item in any specified row and any specified column, we do not find a set of numbers or a group).

For database tables, we add three more properties:

P_3: All rows of a table must be distinct (duplicate rows are not allowed).
P_4: The ordering of rows within a table is immaterial.
P_5: The columns of a table are assigned distinct names, and the ordering of columns within a table is immaterial.

This kind of table is called a *relation*. If it has n columns, then it is called a "relation of degree n."

The column names are called *attributes*. The set of all column names for a table is called a *relation scheme*; and the table is a "relation over the relation scheme." In general, a database consists of more than one table, each having its own set of attributes or column names. The *database scheme* is the collection of all relation schemes of tables in the database. (Two distinct relation schemes may have some column names—attributes—in common.) A table is an *instance* of a relation over a relation scheme; i.e., if we change the data in the table in any way we have a different relation with the same relation scheme. Chapter 11 gives further details on the distinction between a relation scheme and a relation.

The following lines summarize these definitions and relate them to the terms used in this text,

- A relation will denote a table.
- An attribute will be called a *column*.
- A single record will be called a *row*.
- An individual value at the intersection of any row and column will be called a *datum*.

1.4 Properties of Tables

A table name may be preceded by the name of the person who created it, followed by a period. For example, a table called "Personnel" created by Baker may be referred to as "Baker.Personnel" or simply by the name "Personnel."

A table name cannot be a SQL keyword (SQL keywords are listed in Chapter 2.)

There are two types of tables in a relational database: base tables and virtual tables. A *base table* conforms to the definition of a table shown above. A *virtual table*, also called a *view*, exists only as a definition in the catalog. Every time a view is accessed, the definition is retrieved from the catalog and the query in the definition is executed, creating a table with the columns listed in the view definition. A view is called a virtual table because it does not exist in its own right in the database as a base table does. Instead, a view is reconstructed from the data of its underlying base table(s) whenever the view is queried.

While in its simplest form a view may be a portion of a base table, a view can also be the result of joining a portion of one or more tables together. A view can also be a portion of a view, with the latter view being a portion of a base table. Views are discussed in detail in Chapter 9.

Throughout this text, base tables will be called simply *tables* and virtual tables will be called *views*.

1.5 The NULL Value

SQL supports the concept of a NULL value to indicate incomplete or unavailable information. This value can be thought of as simply a place holder in the domain of an attribute.

There are differing opinions about the utility or indeed the logic behind the concept of NULL values, and since it may be instructive to be apprised of these, the following references are offered: Date [27], Lipski [45], Codd [21], and Maier [46].

At the present time, however, NULLs are very much a part of SQL and appear more likely to be modified and embellished than eliminated from its syntax in the future. They serve the purpose of filling in a blank space in the array of data, but they must be used with caution. The following rules apply, and other special uses and cautions about NULLs will be noted in the contexts in which they occur:

- A NULL value is not the same as a zero.
- One NULL value is not necessarily equal to another NULL value.
- A NULL value cannot be used in a SELECT statement.
- Treatment of NULLs by each of the aggregate functions (See Chapter 7) is not uniform.

2

The Components of SQL

A LTHOUGH SQL IS DESCRIBED AS A QUERY LANGUAGE, IT IS ACTUALLY
much more than that because it contains many other capabilities
in addition to querying a database. These include features for defining
the structure of the data, for modifying data in the database, and
for specifying security constraints. Each feature has its own set of
statements that are expressed in, respectively, Data Definition Language
(DDL), Data Manipulation Language (DML), and Data Control Language
(DCL).

An overview of these three features is presented in this chapter.
Further details of the many uses of them appears in Chapters 4,
5, 6, and succeeding chapters.

SQL also contains sets of words and symbols used in specifying
the results of commands. These are called *value expressions*, *logical
operators*, *predicates*, *table expressions*, *aggregate functions*, and
subqueries. The syntax for each of these is exhibited in the sections
that follow. In each case, the details necessary to use them as well
as examples of their use are shown in later chapters.

2.1   The Catalog

A working relational database employing the SQL data language
will also contain a catalog. While the catalog is essential to efficient

use of SQL, its exact form is a system feature, not a part of SQL. The catalog is a system database containing information about base tables, views, access rights, user-ids, etc. that can be queried through the use of SQL SELECT statements. In a relational system, the catalog contains tables of such information, just like the tables containing the database stored and accessed by the user. The makeup of the catalog is implementor-dependent, and therefore cannot be described here. Its purpose is to provide the user with information about the contents of the database. The user usually cannot apply the UPDATE, INSERT INTO or DELETE commands to the catalog because the operation of the database is dependent on it, and therefore any change made by the user could destroy the integrity of the database.

2.2 SQL Commands

The SQL language consists of a set of commands together with rules for using them. Table 2-1 gives the basic SQL commands along with a brief description of each.

2.3 Keywords

The words forming the SQL commands, as well as the qualifying words used with them, are all designated as *keywords*, and are not available to the user as identifiers. In other words, these keywords cannot be used as names of tables, views, or columns without applying special implementor-defined symbols to them that will distinguish them from their keyword counterparts. Table 2-2 lists the SQL keywords.

2.4 Datatypes

SQL supports three major datatypes, character (CHAR), exact numeric (NUMERIC), and approximate numeric (FLOAT), and the subtypes shown in Table 2-3. (Other datatypes, such as DATE, which allow computations to be performed on dates, are supported in some commercial relational databases by their user interfaces to SQL.)

Character strings (type CHAR) may include numbers (e.g., dates, identification numbers, part numbers, etc.); however, no arithmetic operations can be performed on any character strings. All numeric datatypes are numeric, and can be operated on arithmetically.

Some implementations are case-sensitive (i.e., they will distinguish between upper- and lowercase letters) and some are not. In this text, we will assume a case-sensitive implementation, and therefore

Table 2-1. SQL Commands.

Command	Description
/* . . . */	Comment within or before a SQL command
ALTER TABLE	Adds a column to or redefines a column in an existing table (Not in ANSI Standard SQL).
COMMENT	Inserts a comment about a table or column into the data dictionary.
COMMIT	Commits (makes permanent) completed changes to the database.
CREATE INDEX	Creates an index for a table.
CREATE TABLE	Creates a table and defines its columns and other properties.
CREATE VIEW	Defines a view onto one or more tables and/or other views.
DELETE	Deletes rows from a table.
DROP	Deletes a table, index, etc., from the database.
GRANT	Creates user IDs, assigns passwords, grants, database privileges to users, and grants privileges to users with respect to tables or views.
INSERT	Adds new rows to a table or view.
REVOKE	Revokes database privileges or table access privileges from users.
ROLLBACK	In the event of a system failure, rolls back (eliminates) any noncommitted changes so that database integrity may be maintained. Also allows user to remove any incomplete or incorrect entries before they are COMMITted.
SELECT	Selects rows and columns from one or more tables.
UPDATE	Changes the value of one or more fields in a table.

will capitalize the initial letter of proper names in the examples, for example:

```
WHERE city = 'Dallas':
```

2.5 Value Expressions

SQL supports the following value expressions:

Addition	(+)
Subtraction	(−)

Table 2-2. SQL Keywords.

All	And	Any	As	Asc	Authorization
AVG	Begin	Between	By	Char	Character
Check	Close	Commit	Continue	Count	Create
Current	Cursor	Dec	Decimal	Declare	Delete
Desc	Distinct	Double	End	Escape	Exec
Exists	Fetch	Float	For	Found	From
Go	GOTO	Grant	Group	Having	In
Insert	Int	Integer	Into	Is	Like
Max	Min	Module	Not	Null	Numeric
Of	On	Open	Option	Or	Order
Precision	Privileges	Procedure	Public	Real	Rollback
Schema	Section	Select	Set	Smallint	Some
SQL	Sqlcode	Sqlerror	Sum	Table	To
Union	Unique	Update	User	Values	View
Whenever	Where	With	Work		

Table 2-3. SQL Datatypes.

Datatype	Synonym	Description
CHARACTER	CHAR	Character string with specified length.
Exact Numeric:		
NUMERIC		Precision and scale specified.
DECIMAL	DEC	Scale specified and user-specified precision equal to or greater than the user-supplied precision.
INTEGER	INT	User-defined precision and scale 0.
SMALLINT		Scale 0 and user-defined precision no larger than the precision of INT.
Approximate Numeric:		
FLOAT		Binary precision equal to or greater than the value of the user-supplied precision.
REAL		User-defined precision.
DOUBLE PRECISION		User-defined precision greater than that of REAL.

| Multiplication | (×) |
| Division | (÷) |

The use of these expressions will be illustrated in connection with other expressions, functions, and operators in the sections and chapters that follow.

2.6 Logical Connectives

The SQL language also provides for the logical connectives AND, OR, and NOT. These are discussed in Chapter 7 along with MINUS, which is found in some systems.

2.7 Predicates

A *predicate* is a condition that can be evaluated to produce a truth value of "true," "false," or "unknown." This result is achieved by applying the predicate to a given row of a table. The predicates supported by SQL are:

comparison: (= , < >, <, >, < = , = >)
between (. . .BETWEEN . . . AND . . .)
IN, (NOT IN)
LIKE
NULL
quantified (ALL, SOME, ANY)
EXISTS, (NOT EXISTS)

These predicates are discussed and illustrated in Chapter 3.

2.8 The Data Definition Language (DDL)

A database scheme must be specified by a set of definitions. These can be expressed in the SQL Data Definition Language (DDL), which consists of the Data Definition Statements (DDS) CREATE TABLE, CREATE INDEX, ALTER TABLE, DROP TABLE, DROP VIEW, and DROP INDEX. When the DDS are completed with the appropriate clauses and predicates, and executed, the result is a set of tables and indices. The names of these are then stored in the catalog tables.

2.8.1 Creating Tables

Creation of the database must begin with creation of the tables in which the data will be entered. The DDL statement to create a table must contain the column names, their datatypes, and the sizes of the data to be entered. The syntax is as follows:

```
CREATE TABLE tablename
      (column1__name          datatype(datasize)
       column2-name           datatype(datasize)
       . . .
       columnN-name           datatype(datasize));
```

Note that the entire description of the columns is enclosed in parentheses.

2.8.2   Creating an Index

To create an index on a specified table, the SQL command is:

```
CREATE INDEX   indexname
        ON   tablename (column__name);
```

You can CREATE as many indices as you wish on any one table. You can have an index for each column in the table, as well as an index for a combination of columns. How many and what type of indices you create for a given table will depend on the type of queries you expect will be directed to the database and the size of the database. Too many indices can be as great a liability as too few. This will be discussed further in Chapter 9.

2.8.3   Altering Tables

As new situations develop, or new data are presented for the database to store, the original definition of a table may no longer suffice.

SQL allows you to ALTER a table by adding a column to the existing columns. You can also change the column width of an already established column.

To add another column, the syntax is:

```
ALTER TABLE   tablename
        ADD   column__name datatype;
```

To change the column width of an existing column, the syntax is:

```
ALTER TABLE   tablename
     MODIFY   column__name datatype
              new__width;
```

2.8.4 Dropping Tables

To drop a table from the database, use the DROP TABLE command followed by the name of the table:

```
DROP TABLE   tablename;
```

When a table is dropped by the above SQL command, all views and indices defined on that table are automatically dropped.

2.8.5 Dropping Indices

To drop an index, use the SQL DROP INDEX command followed by the name of the index:

```
DROP INDEX   index_name
         ON   tablename;
```

If you have indices with the same name defined on different tables, the ON must be used, as above, to distinguish the index you want to drop.

If there is no other index with that name on any other table, then you don't need to specify the tablename. The following DROP command will be sufficient:

```
DROP INDEX   index_name;
```

When you DROP an index, this does not drop the tables or views on which the index is based.

2.9   The Data Manipulation Language (DML)

After data are loaded into the tables created by the DDL statements presented in the previous section, the Data Manipulation Statements (DMS) will make it possible to perform manipulations on them, including inserting, updating, deleting and querying (by using the SQL SELECT statement).

Creating a view involves manipulating data in tables that are already in the database. Therefore, creating views is discussed in the context of data manipulation, rather than data definition, and appears in Section 2.9.5 below.

The syntax for the basic forms of these operations is illustrated in the sections that follow.

2.9.1 Inserting

Most systems handle the initial loading into the database of large batches of data in a general loading operation. The SQL INSERT statement is usually used to add new individual rows of data to what already exists in the database. The syntax is:

```
INSERT
INTO tablename (column1_name, column2_name, . . .)
VALUES (' value1', ' value2', . . .);
```

If the list of values is in the same sequence as the sequence of the columns in the table, and there is a value for every column in the table, then the list of column names can be omitted. Otherwise, the column names must be specified as shown above. Values inserted must match the datatype of the column into which they are being inserted. CHAR values must be enclosed in single quotes; neither NUM values nor the NULL value are enclosed in quotes.

2.9.2 Updating

The UPDATE command is used to change the values in existing rows. Its general form is:

```
UPDATE     Tablename
SET        column1 = newvalue,
           column2 = newvalue,

           . . .

           columnN = newvalue,
WHERE      condition;
```

The SET clause of the UPDATE command tells which columns to update and what values to change them to.

The UPDATE command operates on all the rows that meet the condition specified by the WHERE clause. The WHERE clause is optional, but if it is omitted, all rows will be updated.

You can update multiple columns in each row with a single UPDATE command by listing multiple columns after the SET clause as shown in the example above.

The WHERE clause in an UPDATE command may contain a subquery. The use of subqueries for this and other purposes is discussed in Chapter 7.

2.9.3 Deleting

The DELETE command is used to remove rows from a table. Its general form is:

```
DELETE
FROM        tablename
WHERE       condition;
```

You cannot delete partial rows; therefore you do not have to specify column names in the DELETE command.

The WHERE clause determines which rows will be removed. The WHERE clause may be complex and may include multiple conditions, connectives, and/or subqueries.

If you want to delete all rows from a table, omit the WHERE clause, and enter the command:

```
DELETE
FROM        tablename;
```

This will remove all rows, leaving only the column specifications and table name.

2.9.4 Retrieval using SELECT

The basic structure of a SQL query consists of the three clauses:

```
SELECT          column1, column2, . . .
FROM            tablename
WHERE           condition;
```

The SELECT clause lists the columns desired in the result of the query, i.e., the target list. This clause corresponds to the projection operation of the relational algebra.

The FROM clause names the table or tables to be scanned in the execution of the expression. The WHERE clause corresponds to the selection predicate of the relational algebra. It consists of a predicate involving columns of the table(s) that appear(s) in the FROM clause.

The SELECT command and the FROM clause are required for every SQL query. They must appear before any other clauses in a query.

The result of a SQL query is always a table.

2.9.5 Creating Views

In large databases containing large tables, it is much more likely that users will work with views than with complete tables. This can be a matter of security in which certain users are granted privileges only on views rather than on the whole table, and/or it may be a matter of convenience in which there is no need to burden a user with having to make complicated queries of a whole table when the user only works with a small segment of it.

To create a view, you SELECT only those columns from the base table (or tables) in which you are interested.

To define a view, you must give the view a name and then state the query containing the column names and specifications that will comprise the view. The syntax is:

```
CREATE VIEW viewname [(view_column_names)]
        AS (query expression);
```

where (query expression) is a SELECT FROM command.

Usually views are not stored. Instead, they are recomputed for each query referring to them. Techniques for reducing the overhead of this recomputation will be considered in Chapter 9.

While most of the SQL operations that can be performed on tables also can be performed on views, some special rules apply to views because their existence is dependent on the base table(s) from which they are drawn. A view may contain columns from only one table, or it may combine selected columns from two or more tables. There are special considerations for updating, inserting, and deleting when the view is drawn from more than one table. These and other special characteristics of views will be discussed in Chapter 9.

2.10 The Data Control Language (DCL)

The Data Control Language (DCL) consists of a group of SQL statements used for granting authorization for data access, for allocating space, for space definitions, and for auditing database use. Some of these commands represent functions of the database administrator (DBA) and will be discussed in that context in Chapter 6, along with those commands available to other users. The SQL DCL commands are: COMMIT, ROLLBACK, GRANT, and REVOKE.

2.11   Table Expressions (Clauses)

Table expressions are clauses that are used to derive tables. The table expressions supported by SQL and their purposes are:

FROM   Names the table(s) from which rows are to be selected.

WHERE   Specifies the condition(s) the selected rows must meet.

GROUP BY   Separates the rows selected into specified groups.

HAVING   States the condition to be satisfied by each displayed group.

ORDER BY   Specifies the order in which the selected rows will be displayed (either individually or within groups).

The FROM clause is necessary to a SQL query; the WHERE, GROUP BY, HAVING, and ORDER BY clauses are all optional.

Table expressions are discussed in detail, with examples, in Chapter 3.

2.12   Aggregate Functions

The aggregate functions of SQL are not contained in the relational algebra, therefore SQL is considered to be more powerful than the relational algebra in this respect [43].

SQL supports the aggregate, or group, functions AVERAGE (AVG), COUNT DISTINCT, COUNT(*), MAXIMUM (MAX), MINIMUM (MIN), and SUM. These are differentiated from other terms (such as GROUP BY) by the fact that each of the aggregate functions returns a single value for the group of rows it operates on. Descriptions of the purposes of the aggregate functions are shown in Table 2-4.

The aggregate functions all return a single value derived by applying a function to the group of values specified in an argument. In some commercial systems, aggregate functions are called *group functions*, or *built-in* functions, whereas the ANSI standard calls them *set functions*, and some authors call them *column functions* (since they reduce a column of scalar values to a single value). The aggregate function goes in the SELECT statement of a query and is followed by the column to which it applies. To avoid confusion,

Table 2-4. Aggregate Functions.

Function	Description
AVERAGE	Averages the specified values in the column. Column must contain numeric values. Argument may be preceded by DISTINCT to eliminate duplicate values.
COUNT	Returns the number of values in the column; datatype is exact numeric with user-defined precision and scale 0. DISTINCT must be specified.
COUNT(*)	Same as COUNT except DISTINCT is not allowed. Counts all rows without eliminating duplicates.
MINIMUM	Returns the smallest value in the column.
MAXIMUM	Returns the largest value in the column.
SUM	Returns the sum of the values in the column. Column must contain numeric values. Argument may be preceded by DISTINCT to eliminate duplicate values.

the column name is enclosed in parentheses. You can use more than one aggregate function in the same SELECT statement. The syntax for using aggregate functions is shown below:

```
SELECT    aggregate_function1(column_name),. . .,
          aggregate-functionN(column_name)
FROM      table(s)
WHERE     condition(s);
```

The aggregate functions are discussed, with examples, in Chapter 7.

2.13 Subqueries

SQL provides for the use of subqueries. (In some database systems, subqueries are called *nested SELECTs*). These can be used to obtain information needed to complete the main query. The use of a subquery results in the writing of one compound query instead of two or more simple queries, and therefore provides a method for increased user efficiency.

In the processing of such a compound SQL statement, the subquery is evaluated first; then the results are applied to the main query. The most powerful uses of SQL can be achieved by users who are skilled in setting up subqueries. SQL imposes no limit on the number of subqueries that may be nested within a query, although the implementor may impose a limit.

If you know that the subquery should return at most only one value, or if you want to be certain that the result is unique the syntax is:

```
SELECT      columns
FROM        tables
WHERE       condition (comparison predicate)
            (subquery);
```

The above syntax will return an error message if more than one row fits the condition.

On the other hand, if the subquery will (or could) return more than one value, then the syntax requires the IN predicate as follows:

```
SELECT      column
FROM        tablesa
WHERE       column_name IN
            (subquery);
```

Further details on constructing subqueries, as well as examples of them, appear in Chapter 7.

3

Table Expressions and Predicates

THE FOLLOWING CLAUSES ARE TABLE EXPRESSIONS USED TO DERIVE tables: FROM, WHERE, GROUP BY, HAVING, and ORDER BY. They are discussed in Sections 3.1 through 3.1.5 below.

The predicates used in SQL to place a specific condition on a query are the following: comparison (= , < > , < , > , < = , > =), BETWEEN, IN, LIKE, NULL, and quantified (ALL, SOME, ANY), and EXISTS. These predicates are explained and illustrated in Sections 3.2 through 3.2.7 below.

3.1 Table Expressions (Clauses)

Table expressions are used to specify a table or a grouped table. These are clauses that are used to derive tables that are the result of the last specified clause. The table expressions are:

FROM
WHERE
GROUP BY
HAVING
ORDER BY

The FROM clause is necessary to a SQL query; the WHERE, GROUP BY, HAVING, and ORDER BY clauses are all optional.

3.1.1 The FROM Clause

The FROM clause specifies a table or tables from which the desired rows are to be retrieved. For example:

```
SELECT      *
FROM        suppliers
```

specifies that rows are to be retrieved with values in all columns from the Suppliers table.

A SQL query always returns a table. Therefore, the result of the FROM clause is always a table. If there are no optional table expressions in the query (i.e., WHERE, GROUP BY, HAVING, or ORDER BY), then the retrieved table is the table composed of the columns in the target list only.

If the table retrieved by the FROM clause is a grouped view, then the query cannot contain any optional table expressions such as WHERE, GROUP BY, or HAVING. (See Chapter 9 for further discussion of this point.)

If the target list contains columns from more than one table, then the FROM clause must name all of those tables in any order, regardless of the order of the columns in the target list.

3.1.2 The WHERE Clause

The WHERE clause specifies a table derived by the application of a search condition to the tables listed in the FROM clause. In other words, the result of a WHERE clause is that row (or rows) retrieved from the tables named in the FROM clause that meets the WHERE clause specification. The syntax is:

```
SELECT      column1, column2, . . . , columnN
FROM        tablename
WHERE       condition;
```

For example, if you wanted to send out a notice only to the salespeople of your firm, you could SELECT the list of salesmen with the following command:

```
SELECT      employee__name, employee#
FROM        employees
WHERE       title = ' salesman';
```

The WHERE clause may contain one or more subqueries. If it does, each subquery following the WHERE clause is executed for each row retrieved by the FROM clause. (Subqueries are defined and discussed in Chapter 7.)

3.1.3 The GROUP BY Clause

The GROUP BY clause specifies a grouped table resulting from the application of the GROUP BY clause to the result of any previously specified clause.

The GROUP BY clause specifically references a column of the table named in the FROM clause and groups rows on the basis of the values in that column.

The result of the GROUP BY clause partitions the result of the FROM clause into a set of groups so that for each group of more than one row, the values in the grouping column are identical. The syntax is:

```
SELECT      column1, column2, . . . , columnN
FROM        tablename
GROUP BY    grouping_column;
```

For example, if a table of suppliers were queried and the result were grouped by city as follows:

```
SELECT      *
FROM        suppliers
GROUP BY    city;
```

the result would be another Suppliers table grouped so that each set retrieved would be a group of suppliers located in the same city, such as

Suppliers Name	Part No.	Part Name	City	Unit Price
Acme	38	Valve	New York	5.00
Ziptools	2	Hose	New York	3.00
Best	15	Filter	Chicago	4.00
Handy	6	Valve	Chicago	3.00
Central	18	Piston	Chicago	8.00

Suppliers Name	Part No.	Part Name	City	Unit Price
Joe's	74	Piston	Wichita	6.00
First	9	Hose	Mobile	2.00
Quiktool	22	Filter	Mobile	4.00
ABC	8	Valve	Mobile	3.00

The GROUP BY clause cannot be used when the table resulting from the FROM clause is a grouped view. (See Chapter 9 for details on views.)

If the command does not contain a WHERE clause, then the GROUP BY clause is placed immediately after the FROM clause. If the command has a WHERE clause, then the GROUP BY clause goes after the WHERE clause.

The rows returned will be ordered randomly within each group because the GROUP BY clause does not do any ordering.

3.1.4   The HAVING Clause

The HAVING clause specifies a restriction on the grouped table resulting from the previous GROUP BY clause and eliminates groups not meeting the condition it specifies. If HAVING is specified in a query, then GROUP BY must also have been specified.

HAVING is used to specify the quality a group must possess for it to be returned. HAVING compares a property of the group with a constant value. It performs the same function for groups that WHERE performs for individual rows. In other words, HAVING eliminates nonqualifying groups, in the same way that WHERE eliminates nonqualifying rows. HAVING is therefore always used with GROUP BY. The syntax is:

```
SELECT      column1, column2, . . . , columnN
FROM        tablename
GROUP BY    grouping_column
HAVING      specified_group_property;
```

For example, if you want to find out the average annual salary for all job titles where there is more than one employee, enter:

```
SELECT      title, COUNT(*), 12 * AVG(salary)
FROM        employees
```

```
GROUP BY      title
HAVING        COUNT(*) > 1;
```

Referring to the table under Section 3.1.3 above, to select only those suppliers who are located in a city in which there are more than two suppliers, set up the query:

```
SELECT      name, city
FROM        suppliers
GROUP BY    city
HAVING      COUNT(*) > 2;
```

The following will be returned:

Name	City
Best	Chicago
Handy	Chicago
Central	Chicago
First	Mobile
Quiktool	Mobile
ABC	Mobile

The HAVING clause is always placed after the GROUP BY clause. Examples of other uses of HAVING are shown in Section 7.2 on aggregate functions and Section 7.4 on subqueries, both in Chapter 7.

3.1.5 The ORDER BY Clause

The ORDER BY clause allows you to specify the order in which rows will appear in the retrieval. Whereas GROUP BY merely places together all rows that have the same value in a specified column, ORDER BY lists the rows within a specified group according to increasing or decreasing value.

If the ORDER BY clause is used, it must be the last clause in a SELECT command.

Ascending (ASC) or descending (DESC) order may be specified, but ASC is the default ordering; therefore it is usually only necessary to specify the direction if DESC is the desired ordering.

If the ordering column consists of letters rather than numbers, SQL will use ascending alphabetic order (starting with A) if DESC is not specified.

For example, the following command can be used to order suppliers alphabetically:

```
SELECT      supplier__name, part#, part__name
FROM        suppliers
ORDER BY    supplier__name;
```

This command would result in an alphabetic ordering of the suppliers starting with those names beginning with A, as shown below:

Suppliers

Name	Part#	Part Name
ABC	8	Valve
Acme	38	Valve
Best	15	Filter
Central	18	Piston
First	9	Hose
Handy	6	Valve
Joe's	74	Piston
Quiktool	22	Filter
Ziptools	2	Hose

You can also ORDER BY more than one column. For example, the above query could be written as follows:

```
SELECT      supplier__name, part#, part__name
FROM        suppliers
ORDER BY    supplier__name, part#;
```

In this case the first ordering will be alphabetical in ASC order, and part numbers will be shown in ASC order within each alphabetical listing. For the list shown above, this two-column ordering would not change the order, but note that listing two ordered columns does affect the next example.

To achieve a descending ordering, put the DESC after the column name. For example, to list suppliers starting with those who sell the most expensive parts and ending with those who sell the least expensive ones, you might use the following query:

```
SELECT      supplier__name, part__name, price
FROM        suppliers
ORDER BY    price DESC, supplier__name;
```

This will list all suppliers by price starting with the highest price and working down to the lowest, and within each price, the suppliers will be ordered alphabetically in ASC order, as shown below:

Suppliers

Supplier Name	Part Name	Price
Central	Piston	8.00
Joe's	Piston	6.00
Acme	Valve	5.00
Best	Filter	4.00
Quiktool	Filter	4.00
ABC	Valve	3.00
Handy	Valve	3.00
Ziptools	Hose	3.00
First	Hose	2.00

3.2 Predicates

Predicates are conditions that are stated in the WHERE clause of a SQL query. The predicates supported by SQL are Comparison, BETWEEN, IN, LIKE, NULL, quantified, and EXISTS; each of these is discussed and illustrated in the sections that follow.

3.2.1 The Comparison Predicate

A comparison predicate specifies a comparison of two values. It consists of a value expression followed by a comparison operator followed by either another value expression or a single-valued subquery. The datatypes of the two value expressions, or the value expression and the subquery, must be comparable. The comparison operators supported by SQL are:

equals	=
not equal to	< >
less than	<
greater than	>
less than or equal to	< =
greater than or equal to	> =

If the values on both sides of a comparison operator are not NULL, then the comparison predicate is either true or false. For example:

```
321003 < > 123003
'March 21, 1988'  =  'March 21, 1988'
520 > 519
0 < 2
```

If either of the two value expressions is a NULL value, or if the subquery is empty, then the result of the comparison predicate is unknown; however, when GROUP BY, ORDER BY, or DISTINCT are used in conjunction with a comparison predicate, one NULL value is identical to, or is a duplicate of, another NULL value.

Character strings may be compared by means of the above comparison operators. This is accomplished by comparing characters in the same ordinal positions in the string. Thus, two character strings are equal if all characters with the same ordinal position are equal. For example,

```
'London'  =  'London'
'London' < > 'New York'
'52-I-432' < > '521432FM
```

3.2.2 The BETWEEN Predicate

The BETWEEN predicate specifies a range comparison. The syntax is:

. . . BETWEEN . . . AND . . .

or

. . . NOT BETWEEN . . . AND . . .

where each ellipsis contains a value. The datatypes of the values must be comparable.

For example, to select parts priced between $5 and $10, enter:

```
SELECT part#, part_name, price, supplier
   FROM           suppliers
   WHERE          price BETWEEN 5 AND 10;
```

The above query will return the following:

PART#	PART_NAME	PRICE	SUPPLIER
74	piston	6	Joe's
38	valve	5	Acme
18	piston	8	Central

(Note that since no ordering was specified, the rows returned will be in random order. The same query entered again in exactly the same way might return a different random order.)

The term NOT may also be used with BETWEEN to retrieve information outside of a range rather than inside the range. For example, to retrieve information only on parts priced below $3.00 and above $6.00, enter:

```
SELECT      part#, part__name, price, supplier
FROM        suppliers
WHERE       price NOT BETWEEN 3 AND 6;
```

This query would return:

PART#	PART NAME	PRICE	SUPPLIER
9	hose	2	First
18	piston	8	Central

3.2.3   The IN (or NOT IN) Predicate

The IN (or NOT IN) predicate specifies a quantified comparison. It lists a set of values and tests for whether or not a candidate value is in that list. The list must be enclosed in parentheses.

For example, to retrieve those parts whose price is any of the following: $4, $5, $7, enter

```
SELECT      part#, part__name, price, supplier
FROM        suppliers
WHERE       price IN (4,5,7);
```

The result will be:

PART#	PART NAME	PRICE	SUPPLIER
15	filter	4	Best
22	filter	4	Quiktool
38	valve	5	Acme

We could have written this query using OR instead of IN, as follows:

```
SELECT        part#, part_name, price, supplier
FROM          suppliers
WHERE         price = 4
OR            price = 5
OR            price = 7;
```

The resulting retrieval would be the same as shown above for the query using IN.

The query can also be written using ANY:

```
SELECT        part#, part_name, price, supplier
FROM          suppliers
WHERE         price = ANY (4, 5, 7);
```

Again, the resulting retrieval would be the same as shown above for the query using IN.

The order in which the items in the list are shown in the query determines the order in which the columns will be displayed in the retrieval. It does not determine the order in which the rows will be displayed. If you want the retrieved rows to appear in a specific order, then the WHERE clause must be followed by an ORDER BY clause indicating the column variable on which the ordering should be based.

The spaces between the items in the list are optional and will not affect the result.

The IN predicate can be negated by the use of NOT IN. For example, to obtain part numbers other than those contained in the set 4, 5, and 7, enter

```
SELECT    part#, part_name, price, supplier
FROM      suppliers
WHERE     price IN (4,5,7);
```

The resulting retrieval will return every existing part number except parts numbered 4, 5, and 7.

3.2.4   The LIKE (or NOT LIKE) Predicate

The LIKE predicate specifies a pattern-matching comparison in which an underscore (_) is used to represent a single character in the pattern, and a percent sign (%) is used to represent a character string of arbitrary length (including zero). These symbols are sometimes called *wild cards* or *don't care* symbols. They are used in cases in which the information is incomplete.

The form of the LIKE predicate is:

column__name LIKE *character__string__constant*

LIKE can only be used with character string or graphic data, not with numeric data.

For example, if you need the name and address of a supplier and are uncertain whether the company name is Reid or Read, you can enter:

```
SELECT      name, city
FROM        suppliers
WHERE       name LIKE ' Re__d';
```

The use of the underscore indicates uncertainty on only one character.

If you are unsure whether the name is Redenbacker or Redinburger, then you should use the percent sign (%):

```
SELECT      name, city
FROM        suppliers
WHERE       name LIKE ' Red%';
```

To reduce the vast number of retrievals that might occur with the above query, enter:

```
SELECT      name, city
FROM        suppliers
WHERE       name LIKE ' Red__nb%er';
```

The above indicates certainty on the position of the 'n' but uncertainty on the one letter between the 'd' and the 'n', certainty on the 'b' following the 'n' and uncertainty on the number and identity of the characters before the final 'er'.

These two symbols can be used in a wide variety of ways, either individually or in combination with each other. They can also be used with NOT, which will exclude retrievals taking a certain form. For example, if we are looking for a name that we know does not include the character string 'del,' the predicate can be expressed as:

```
WHERE name NOT LIKE ' %del%'
```

This would exclude a name with that exact combination of letters, in that order, regardless of where 'del' occurred in the name. It would not, however, exclude the possibility that any of the individual letters 'd,' 'e,' or 'l,' might occur within the name. To exclude the occurrence of any of the individual letters in the retrieved name, we would have to exclude them individually because the clause shown above will only exclude that exact character string.

3.2.5   The NULL Predicate

The NULL predicate specifies a test for a NULL value. To query the database about a NULL value requires a slightly different approach than querying about any other value because of the special properties embodied in the NULL concept.

For example, if we are looking for a part name where, because of incomplete information, the price has been entered as NULL, we cannot specify

```
WHERE price = NULL
```

because nothing, not even NULL itself, is equal to the NULL value. (This rule does not always hold throughout the SQL syntax. See, for example, the treatment of NULL values with SELECT DISTINCT, UNIQUE, and ORDER BY.)

Also, SQL does not allow NULL to be used in a SELECT clause.

You cannot find the NULL value by exclusion, as, for example, by stipulating that the price is above or below any known price in the list. For example, if $10 is the highest specified price in the list, the query

```
SELECT      part_name, price
FROM        suppliers
WHERE       price > 10;
```

would not retrieve the part name with the NULL value, nor would the predicate

```
WHERE price < 0
```

The only predicate allowed when searching for a NULL value is:

```
WHERE column_specification IS NULL.
```

To exclude a NULL value, the syntax is:

WHERE *column__specification* IS NOT NULL.

Therefore, to retrieve the names of suppliers for whom the price of the part supplied has been entered in the database as NULL, enter:

```
SELECT      supplier__name
FROM        suppliers
WHERE       price IS NULL;
```

To retrieve the names of the suppliers for whom the price of the part has been entered in the database as a value other than NULL, enter:

```
SELECT      supplier__name
FROM        suppliers
WHERE       price IS NOT NULL;
```

No other syntax will retrieve the desired target list when the NULL predicate is involved.

3.2.6 The Quantified Predicates: ALL, SOME, ANY

The quantified predicates ALL, SOME, and ANY require the use of a comparison predicate applied to the results of a subquery. A comparison predicate is a predicate containing a comparison operator such as equals (=), less than (<), greater than (>), less than or equal to (< =), greater than or equal to (> =), and not equal (< >), as explained in Section 3.2.1 above.

These predicates allow us to test a single value against all of the members of a set. For example, you might want to find the suppliers whose prices are lower than all the suppliers in Chicago. To do so, enter:

```
SELECT      supplier__name
FROM        suppliers
WHERE       price < ALL
            (SELECT    price
             FROM      suppliers
             WHERE     city = 'Chicago');
```

Similarly, all the other comparison operators may be combined with SOME, ANY, and ALL. When the comparison operator being used is equals (=), the term ANY is interchangeable with IN, and it sometimes may seem more logical to use the IN.

In many cases ANY has the same meaning as SOME. Consider the query, "Find all suppliers with a price lower than some supplier in Chicago." You can write this as:

```
SELECT          supplier__name
FROM            suppliers
WHERE           price < ANY
        (SELECT         price
        FROM            suppliers
        WHERE           city = 'Chicago');
```

The < ANY comparison in the WHERE clause of the outer SELECT is true if the price is less than at least one member of the set of all suppliers in Chicago.

3.2.7   The EXISTS Predicate

The EXISTS predicate states the condition(s) for an empty set. It contains a subquery (see Chapter 7, Section 7.4, for a discussion of subqueries) which together with the stipulation EXISTS can be evaluated to either true or false. If the result of the subquery EXISTS, then the predicate is true. If the result of the subquery does not EXIST, then the set described by the subquery is empty.

From the above paragraph it is apparent that the predicate EXISTS represents the existential quantifier of formal logic.

The universal quantifier of formal logic, FORALL, is not directly supported by the SQL language; it will be shown, however, that an equivalent predicate using EXISTS will produce the same result as that which could be obtained with FORALL.

The predicate EXISTS can be used wherever a query using the predicate IN can be used. (But the inverse is not true, i.e., IN cannot always be used where EXISTS is appropriate.) Since queries using EXISTS are sometimes easier to formulate than queries using IN, the use of EXISTS takes on added importance in SQL.

The general syntax for the EXISTS predicate is:

```
SELECT          column_name
FROM            tablename
WHERE           EXISTS (subquery);
```

Only the general form of the EXISTS subquery is shown here, with further details appearing in Chapter 7.

A query may also be phrased using NOT EXISTS with the same syntax. NOT can be added after the WHERE in the outer SELECT:

```
WHERE NOT EXISTS
            (SELECT*
            FROM tablename
            WHERE          condition(s) );
```

The predicate form NOT EXISTS may also be used to obtain the result that can be obtained with the universal quantifier FORALL, which is not available in SQL. It involves use of the double negative:

```
NOT (EXISTS variable (NOT (variable contained in constant)))
```

Since this is best explained by the use of an alias, it will be exhibited in Chapter 7, Section 7.3.1, where aliases are explained.

Exercises

3.1 Write a SQL query to retrieve all columns and rows of the customer and supplier tables.

3.2 Write the FROM clause, and wherever necessary the WHERE clause and/or other table expressions, for each of the following:

A. For suppliers with a price lower than $5.
B. For a list of all suppliers, with the part numbers in ASC order.
C. For suppliers of valves, in alphabetical order.
D. For a customer whose name starts with H and ends with y.
E. For a supplier whose name is either Quiktool or Quicktool.
F. For suppliers in New York, Atlanta, or Denver.
G. For part numbers 8, 9, or 10.
H. For suppliers for whom the part number has been entered as NULL.

I. For suppliers for whom the part number has been filled in with a value other than NULL.

Answers to Exercises

3.1 SELECT *
FROM customer, suppliers;

3.2

A. FROM suppliers
WHERE price < 5;
B. FROM suppliers
ORDER BY part#;
C. FROM suppliers
WHERE part__name = 'valves'
ORDER BY supplier__name;
D. FROM customers
WHERE supplier__name = 'H%y';
E. FROM suppliers
WHERE supplier__name = 'Qui%ktool';
F. FROM suppliers
WHERE supplier__name IN ('New York', 'Atlanta', 'Denver');
G. FROM suppliers
WHERE part# BETWEEN '8' AND '10';
H. FROM suppliers
WHERE part# IS NULL;
I. FROM suppliers
WHERE part# IS NOT NULL;

4

Using the Data Definition Statements

THE FOLLOWING PRACTICAL APPLICATION OF THE DATA DEFINITION statements will assume that you are using any operating system and a user-interface capable of executing the SQL statements.

We will use SQL commands to set up a small database, and in succeeding chapters will enlarge upon and extend its capabilities. The procedures will apply to a database of any size. The progressive development will illustrate the use of SQL from the standpoint of a one-service (or product), single-user system on through a multiuser database management system for a multiproduct, multiservice organization.

Since a relational database consists of tables, and from the user's viewpoint, nothing but tables, the first task is to create those tables. Operating system or user-interface pathways to create and/or access tables will not be discussed in this text. The construction of more complex SQL statements that will optimize existing search routes, however, will be exhibited in Chapter 9.

The design of the database, an important topic in its own right, will not be considered here, because employment of the SQL commands will be the same regardless of how the system is designed. This text will assume that an appropriate design has been worked out for the situation at hand.

4.1   The CREATE TABLE Command

A base table is defined and created with the following syntax:

CREATE TABLE *tablename*
    Column definition(s)
    Optional UNIQUE constraint
Optional NOT NULL constraint

where *column definition* contains each column name along with the datatype for that column, and the constraint definitions, if any, may be NOT NULL or UNIQUE or both.

If UNIQUE is specified, then that column cannot contain any duplicate values. If NOT NULL is specified, then a value other than NULL must be filled in for every row in that column. If UNIQUE is specified for any column, then NOT NULL must also be specified for that column.

If both UNIQUE and NOT NULL are specified, these two constraints on a column make the column eligible for use as a primary key. (Primary keys are discussed in Chapter 9.)

For the purpose of illustrating the SQL syntax in this and succeeding chapters, assume we are working with a company whose initial function is to sell automobile replacement parts. The company has four employees: the owner, a secretary, and two salesmen. We will work with the owner to transform his paper files to a relational database management system using SQL as its query language.

The company buys the parts in quantity from each manufacturer and resells them individually to automobile repair shops. We have determined that we need the following:

1. A table containing the names and addresses of parts suppliers, and listing the part numbers and part names of the items they supply, and the price of those parts.

2. A table containing the names and addresses of repair shops (customers) and listing what they have ordered from us, what they owe us, and the due date of their payment.

3. A list of our personnel, their Social Security numbers, their addresses, their salaries, any commissions paid to them, and their job titles.

These three tables will get us started; when we need more tables or more columns in these tables, the relational form of the database will allow us to make additions at any time without disrupting the operation or compromising the database.

The syntax shown in Chapter 2 for creating any table is:

CREATE TABLE *tablename*
    (*Column1_name*   *datatype, datasize*
    Column2_name   *datatype, datasize*
    . . .
    ColumnN-name   *datatype, datasize)*;

The datatype of each column must be specified in the CREATE statement. The types of data supported by SQL are shown in Table 2-3.

Therefore, we will set up the first table as follows:

CREATE TABLE Suppliers
    (Name   CHAR(30) NOT NULL
    Address   CHAR(30) NOT NULL
    Part#   CHAR(12) UNIQUE NOT NULL
    Part_name   CHAR(15)
    Price   NUM(11));

The above will give us a table in which 30 CHAR spaces are allowed for the supplier's name, 30 CHAR spaces for the supplier's address, 12 CHAR spaces for recording the supplier's part number, 15 CHAR spaces for the part name, and 11 NUMerical spaces for the price of the part. (CHAR spaces are used for the part number because these numbers are merely labels and cannot be used with arithmetic operations, and using CHAR will allow the use of letters that may accompany the numbers of some parts.)

Notice that the NOT NULL constraint on the Name column and on the Address column ensures that if a supplier's name is entered, the address must also be entered, and vice versa. The UNIQUE NOT NULL specification on the Part No. column ensures not only that this column will not be left blank, but also that there is no duplication of part numbers. (Therefore, Part No. could serve as a primary key.) The part name and the price do not have to be entered when Name, Address, and Part No. are entered because there is no NOT NULL specification on those columns.

The above table will be too wide to fit on the 80-column screen of most CRTs. Therefore, it will not be possible to see the whole table at once; it will have to be scrolled horizontally, which may become inconvenient when entering orders. For the moment we will let this problem stand and consider it in an exercise at the end of the chapter.

Now, we must set up the table listing our customers.

```
CREATE TABLE customers
    (Name            CHAR(30)NOT NULL
    Address          CHAR(30)NOT NULL
    Part#            CHAR(12)
    Part__Name       CHAR(15)
    Price            NUM(10)
    Due__Date        NUM(10));
```

As with the supplier table, this table will contain a Name column with a maximum CHAR width of 30 spaces, a Customer Address column with a CHAR width of 30 spaces, a Part No. column with a CHAR width of 12 spaces, a Part Name column with a CHAR width of 15 spaces, a Price column with a NUMerical width of 10 spaces, and a Due Date column with a NUMerical width of 10 spaces. The NOT NULL constraint on the Customer Name and Address columns specify that those columns cannot be left blank. Therefore, if any item in a row is filled in, the Customer Name and Address must be filled in.

Again, we have the problem of a table that extends so far horizontally that it will be necessary for the user to scroll over to see it all. This brings with it the same problem as the suppliers table brought. Again, we will leave this problem to be resolved in the exercises at the end of the chapter.

The few employees of this company would hardly need a table were it not for the need to file periodic government reports on amounts paid to them. Also, an employee may leave during the year and be replaced by another employee. Therefore, at the end of any year, the employee table may contain several more names than the number actually working at the company on that date. Our year-end reports must include everyone employed during the year whether or not they are still on the payroll. The table must allow for this. Therefore, we will set it up as follows:

```
CREATE TABLE employees
    (Name            CHAR(50)
    Address          CHAR(50)
    SS#              CHAR(12) UNIQUE NOT NULL
    Title            CHAR(10)
```

```
Salary                      NUM(8)
Commission                  NUM(8));
```

The UNIQUE NOT NULL constraint on the SS# column will prevent the entry of the same SS# for two different employees as well as ensuring that this column is never left blank.

No two columns in the same table can have the same name although two columns in different tables may have the same name.

The table's name may be preceded by the *authorization identifier* (id) of the person who created the table. The authorization identifier is the name the person uses in logging onto the database. (See Chapter 6 for details on authorization identifiers.) When an id is used, it is separated from the table name by a period (.); for example:

```
CREATE TABLE baker.employees
```

would create an employees table owned by the user whose id is Baker.

It may sometimes be necessary to move a set of data from an existing table to another table that has been set up for some special purpose. In this case, it is possible to set up the new table and transfer the desired set of data all with one command. The syntax for doing this is:

```
CREATE TABLE        new_tablename (column1, column2,
                    . . . columnN)
AS                  (SELECT      column1, column2, . . .
                                 columnN)
                    FROM         old_tablename
                    WHERE        condition);
```

The SQL statement following the word AS is a subquery designating the information to be taken from the existing table. You do not need to specify datatypes or sizes for the new table because these will be determined by the datatypes and sizes of the columns in the existing table.

Assume, for example, that you might want a special confidential list of the customers who have not paid their bill within 60 days after the due date, so that these names can be turned over to a collection agency. To set up this new table, which we will call Deadbeats, and put the nonpaying customers accounts into it, enter:

```
CREATE TABLE      deadbeats   (name, address, amount, due__date)
AS                (SELECT     name, address, amount, due__date
                  FROM   customers
                  WHERE  due__date < =  current   - 60);
```

Note the use of the value expression minus (–) in the WHERE clause of the subquery. This assumes that the implementation you are using includes a method for applying value expressions to dates and a method for subtracting one date from another. Such a capability is not contained within SQL, but it is usually a part of the implementation.

The above command will set up the new Deadbeats table, and copy into it all rows in the Customers Table in which the account is 60 or more days overdue. This command does not remove the specified rows from the Customers Table. To remove them you must enter a DELETE command, as explained in Chapter 5.

4.2   The CREATE VIEW Command

To create a view, you use the same initial command as that used to create a table, but from there on, the process is slightly different for two reasons:

- The columns are already set up in the table from which the view will be taken; therefore the column datatype and width in the view will be whatever they are in the base table and will not have to be specified in the CREATE VIEW command.
- To set up a view, you must SELECT the columns you want out of the base table(s). Selecting columns amounts to manipulating the data rather than defining it, and this operation comes under the rules for data manipulation. These will be explained in Chapter 5.

The general syntax for creating a view is:

```
CREATE VIEW viewname [(view__column__names)]
AS          (SELECT column(s)
            FROM  table(s)
            WHERE condition(s));
```

The specifics for selecting the columns are discussed in Section 5.5 in Chapter 5.

4.3 The CREATE INDEX Command

CREATE and DROP are the only SQL operations on indices available to an end user. These are all that are needed because decisions about using specific indices for optimal retrieval paths should be made by the system rather than by the user. However, the number and type of indices available to the system may influence retrieval speed. Therefore this subject is treated in more detail in Chapter 9. To CREATE an index, use the command:

```
CREATE INDEX index_name
ON tablename;
```

4.4 The ALTER TABLE Command

The 1986 version of the ANSI standard for SQL does not contain a provision for altering a table with the ALTER command; however, this is a useful SQL command, which is employed in most commercial databases using SQL. Therefore it will be illustrated here as it is presented in *ORACLE*.

It was pointed out earlier that a relational database can be easily altered to accommodate the changing needs of a database over time. In this context the ALTER TABLE command provides one way to make changes. It has two forms: ALTER TABLE. . .ADD and ALTER TABLE. . .MODIFY.

These two ALTER commands can be used to add a new column to an existing table, to increase or decrease a column size, to change the datatype of a column, to add a NOT NULL specification to a column, or to remove a NOT NULL specification from a column.

Rules covering the use of ALTER TABLE commands ensure that their use does not compromise the integrity of the database. Therefore, in making the changes listed above, the SQL command ALTER TABLE can be used only as follows:

1. To add a column to the existing columns in a table, the syntax is:

```
ALTER TABLE tablename
     ADD columnname datatype(datasize)
```

2. To increase the size of an existing column, the syntax is:

> ALTER TABLE *tablename*
>   MODIFY *columnname (datatype)*
>   *(new_datasize)*;

3. To decrease the size of an existing column (but ONLY IF all rows of that column have the value NULL), the syntax is:

> ALTER TABLE *tablename*
>   MODIFY *columnname (datatype)*
>   *(new_datasize)*;

4. To change the datatype of an existing column (but *only if* all rows of that column have the value NULL at the time the datatype is changed), the syntax is:

> ALTER TABLE *tablename*
>   MODIFY *columnname*
>   *(new_datatype)(new_datasize)*;

5. The NOT NULL specification can *only* be used with the ALTER TABLE command if the column being altered contains no rows. The syntax is:

> ALTER TABLE *tablename*
>   MODIFY *columnname (datatype)(datasize)* NOT
>   NULL;

Obviously this restriction on the use of the NOT NULL specification is to avoid destroying the integrity of the database by setting up a NOT NULL column where some rows have already been filled in with NULL values.

6. A column may be changed from NOT NULL to include NULL values with the following ALTER TABLE command:

> ALTER TABLE *tablename*
>   MODIFY *columnname*
>   *(datatype)(datasize)*NULL;

This use of ALTER TABLE effectively removes a NOT NULL constraint placed on the column earlier.

ALTERing a table changes only the current and future versions of the table. It does not change the way it was represented in the database in the past.

Note that there is no ALTER VIEW command in SQL.

4.5 The DROP TABLE Command

To remove a table from the database, use the DROP TABLE command followed by the name of the table, as follows:

```
DROP TABLE tablename;
```

Dropping a table drops all views defined on that table. It will also drop any indexes defined on that table. Therefore, you should use the DROP TABLE command only after you consider its effect on the rest of the database.

4.6 The DROP VIEW Command

You can use the DROP command to drop views as well as tables:

```
DROP VIEW viewname;
```

Dropping a view does not drop the table from which the view was derived, but it does drop the view from the index.

4.7 The DROP INDEX Command

To drop an index, use the DROP INDEX command followed by the name of the index:

```
DROP INDEX index_name;
```

Since it is possible to have two indices with the same name on different tables, it is safest to specify the name of the table for which the index is being dropped, like this:

```
DROP INDEX index_name
ON tablename;
```

Dropping an index does not drop the tables or views on which the index is based, but dropping an index may affect the access paths by which information can be retrieved by the system. Therefore, you should consider the effect on optimum use of the database before dropping an index.

Exercises

4.1 Suggest a solution to the problem posed in Section 4.1 regarding the horizontal size of the Supplier table and the Customer table.

4.2 Set up a table of prospective customers, called Prospects, which contains their names, addresses, phone numbers when available, and the salesmen assigned to them.

4.3 What is the purpose of the stipulation that a column must contain only NULL values if the ALTER . . . .MODIFY command is used to decrease the column size?

4.4 What is the purpose of the stipulation that a column must have no rows in it if the NOT NULL specification is added with the ALTER. . .MODIFY command?

4.5 Increase the width of the Part# column in the customer table and change it to NUM datatype.

4.6 a. Make up a table called Wimbleton of customers who live in that area, and put those customers' names and addresses in it all with one command.

b. What would be the advantage of creating a view called Wimbleton rather than a table?

4.7 Add a column to the table you made up in Exercise 4.6 to show the telephone numbers of the Wimbleton customers.

4.8 Remove the deadbeats table from the database.

4.9 Enlarge the name column in the customers table to a character string of length 40.

4.10 Write a command to make certain that no user in the company will leave the Due Date blank in the customers table.

Answers to Exercises

4.1 CREATE a view for each showing only those columns needed for specific purposes.

4.2　CREATE TABLE prospects

　　　(name　　　　　CHAR(30)UNIQUE NOT NULL
　　　address　　　　CHAR(35)
　　　phone　　　　　CHAR(12)
　　　salesman　　　 CHAR(20));

4.3　Values already in the table may exceed the reduced column size.

4.4　A row with a NULL value entry may already exist in that column.

4.5　ALTER TABLE customers
　　　　MODIFY part# (NUM)(20);

4.6　a.　CREATE TABLE wimbleton
　　　　　AS　(SELECT name, address
　　　　　FROM　　customers
　　　　　WHERE　address = 'Wimbleton');

　　　b.　A view would reflect future changes in the customers table
　　　　　(such as UPDATEs) whereas a separate table would not.

4.7　ALTER TABLE wimbleton
　　　ADD phone CHAR(12)

4.8　DROP TABLE deadbeats;

4.9　ALTER TABLE customers
　　　MODIFY　(name)(CHAR)(40);

4.10　ALTER TABLE customers
　　　 MODIFY　(due__date) NOT NULL;

5

Using the Data
Manipulation Statements

A S SOON AS THE BASE TABLES ARE SET UP, YOU CAN BEGIN TO INSERT data into the database, update it, change it, delete it, and query it. All of these operations come under the general class of data manipulation.

This chapter will explain and illustrate the basic data manipulation commands. Later chapters will show how these commands can be used in conjunction with other SQL statements to query the database, to optimize retrieval, and to perform more complicated operations.

The data manipulation commands discussed in this chapter are:

INSERT
UPDATE
DELETE
SELECT
CREATE VIEW

5.1   The INSERT Command

The INSERT command is used to put rows or parts of rows into tables. There are two commonly used general forms:

INSERT
INTO   *tablename (column1__name, column2__name, . . .)*

VALUES   (*' value1', ' value2', . . .*);

This form is used when you insert a single row or part of a single row.

INSERT
INTO   *tablename (column1__name, column2__name, . . .)*
             (subquery);

In this second form, the result of evaluating the (subquery) is inserted into the listed columns of the named table. This form is usually used when multiple rows are being inserted. Examples are shown under Section 5.1.2 below.

Any value inserted must match the datatype of the column into which the insertion is being made.

Character values inserted must be enclosed in single quotes as shown above. NULL and numerical values should not be enclosed in quotes.

5.1.1 Inserting All or Part of a Single Row

If values are being inserted into all columns in the table, then column names do not have to be listed after the tablename. The column values being inserted, however must appear in the same order as the order in which the column names were listed when the table was created, with no omitted values. In this case, the syntax is:

INSERT
INTO   *tablename*
VALUES   (*' value1', ' value2', ' value3', . . .*);

For example, to insert the secretary, Ms. Baker, into the employee table created in Chapter 4, filling in all columns in the table, the command would be:

INSERT
INTO   Employees
VALUES   (' Baker', ' Ourtown', ' 21-9990', ' Sec', 900);

The above command inserts a row that stores the following information: Baker, whose address is Ourtown whose Social Security number is 21-9990, whose title is secretary, and whose salary is $900.

If you are inserting fewer column values than the number of columns in the table, then you must either specify column names or insert a NULL value for the column where you are not making an insert—given that that column does not have a NOT NULL specification. In this case, the syntax is:

```
INSERT
INTO        tablename (column1_name, column3_name)
VALUES      (' value1', ' value3');
```

or

```
INSERT
INTO        tablename
VALUES      (' value1', NULL, ' value3');
```

For example, we can insert some of the information for one of our salesmen (Charles) even though we do not know his address or salary at this time by using

```
INSERT      Name, SS#, Title
INTO        Employees
VALUES      (' Charles', ' 31-9999', ' Salesman');
```

where the columns being filled are specified after the INSERT, or

```
INSERT
INTO        Employees
VALUES      (' Charles', NULL, ' 31-9999', ' Salesman', NULL,);
```

where no columns are specified after INSERT, but following VALUES, all columns are accounted for, in the left-to-right order in which they were originally placed in the table; they are represented either by a specific value or by a NULL value.

Both of the entries above indicate that we know Charles' name, but not his address; we know his Social Security number (if we did not know his Social Security number we could not make any entry for him because we cannot insert a NULL value for Social Security number) and his title, but we do not know his salary.

If one column in a table contains a NOT NULL specification, then you cannot fill in any of the columns in that table until you have a value for the NOT NULL column; however, you may fill in one or more of the other columns with NULL.

For example, assume that the company has just agreed to work with Acme, a new supplier in Chicago. We do not yet know the part number Acme assigns to its carburetors or their price. Therefore we cannot INSERT any values for this supplier, since our CREATE TABLE statement (Chapter 4, Section 4.1) specified that part# must be NOT NULL. After we learn that the part# is 4321, we can INSERT the information we have into the Suppliers table:

```
INSERT
INTO        suppliers
VALUES      ('Acme', 'Chicago', '4321', 'carburetor', NULL);
```

This will leave the Price blank, while it fills in the other four columns.

If a column value is specified, and no values are listed for unspecified columns, then SQL will assume that every column is to be filled with a value, and will insert NULLs in place of any unspecified column value—unless that column has a NOT NULL specification. If the column has a NOT NULL specification, and no value is provided, the entry will be rejected.

In the Acme example above, we could have omitted the NULL value, and SQL would have filled it in if we had specified the columns for which we are supplying values, as in the following:

```
INSERT
INTO        suppliers (name, address, part#, part__name)
VALUES      ('Acme', 'Chicago', '4321', 'carburetor');
```

It should be pointed out that omitting column names in the INSERT statement can cause problems if the number or order of the column names has changed since they were listed in the original CREATE TABLE statement. For example, if a column that once allowed a NULL value has been altered in the meantime and a NOT NULL specification added, the entry may be rejected. Assuming that the number and order of column names will remain constant is especially risky within an application program.

5.1.2 Inserting Multiple Rows or Parts of Multiple Rows

The multiple-row INSERT statement shown in Section 5.1 above selects information already in one table and inserts it INTO another table. For example, if we are no longer doing business with Chicago suppliers, and want to pull them out of our current suppliers table yet retain their records, we can CREATE a new table called former suppliers, and put the Chicago suppliers in it. This can be done with the following commands:

```
CREATE TABLE former__suppliers
    (name,      CHAR(10)
     part#      NUM(5)
     price      NUM(10));
```

and

```
INSERT
INTO        former__suppliers (name, part#, price)
            (SELECT     name, part#, price
             FROM       suppliers
             WHERE      city = 'Chicago');
```

The result of the INSERT command will be entered into the new table called Former Suppliers. The above does not remove the Chicago suppliers from the current Suppliers table, however; it merely copies their records into the Former Suppliers table. To remove the Chicago suppliers from the current Suppliers table, use the DELETE command illustrated in Section 5.3 below.

5.2 The UPDATE Command

The UPDATE command is used to change values in existing rows. The general form is:

```
UPDATE      tablename
SET         column1 = newvalue
            column2 = newvalue
            column3 = newvalue
WHERE       condition;
```

When it is used with the UPDATE command, the SET clause indicates which columns are to be updated and what the new values in those columns will be. It is used to impose a condition on all rows specified in the WHERE clause. This avoids having to update each row individually.

For example, let's give the secretary a raise from 900 to 1000 and change her title to Administrative Assistant. The command to do this will be:

```
UPDATE      Employees
SET         title = adm__asst
```

```
                salary  =  1000
WHERE           name  =  ' Baker';
```

The UPDATE command affects all the rows that meet the condition stated in the WHERE clause. If the WHERE clause is omitted, all rows will be updated, for example, if the above UPDATE contained only the following:

```
UPDATE          Employees
SET             Title  =  ' adm__asst'
                Salary  =  1000;
```

then every employee listed in the Employees table would have his/her title changed to Administrative Assistant, and his/her salary changed to $1000 regardless of what values these columns had before the UPDATE.

You can update several rows at once by specifying conditions in the WHERE clause that will apply to those rows.

As shown above in the general form of the UPDATE command, you can update several columns in each row with a single UPDATE command by listing those columns after the word SET. For example, suppose we wanted to give all salesmen listed in our employees table a 10 percent raise. We can do this with one command as follows:

```
UPDATE          employees
SET             salary  =  1.1 * salary
WHERE           title  =  ' salesman';
```

The WHERE clause in an UPDATE command may contain a subquery; for example:

```
UPDATE          tablename
SET             salary  =  1.1 * salary
WHERE           commission  =
            (subquery)
```

This is shown in greater detail in Section 7.4 of Chapter 7, where subqueries are illustrated.

5.3 The DELETE Command

To remove rows from a table, use the DELETE command. The syntax is as follows:

```
DELETE
FROM        tablename
WHERE       condition;
```

You cannot delete partial rows; therefore it is not necessary to include the column names. The condition stated in the WHERE clause will determine which rows are deleted. To delete one row from a table, specify a condition in the WHERE clause applying to just that row. To delete several rows from a table (all with one command) specify the condition common to all of the rows. To delete all the rows from a table (all with one command) omit the WHERE clause and enter only the command:

```
DELETE FROM tablename;
```

This command will remove all of the rows from the table, leaving only the column specifications and tablename. Note that this differs from the DROP command, which would remove the tablename and column specifications as well as all rows.

5.4   The SELECT Command

To query the database and retrieve information from it, use the SELECT command. The general form of the SELECT command is:

```
SELECT      column1, column2, column3, . . .
FROM        tablename;
```

If there is more than one column specified after the SELECT, these columns must be separated by a comma.

Columns are returned in the order specified in the SELECT statement, not in the order in which they were originally entered into the table when it was created.

If you want to see entries in all columns of a table, use the asterisk after the SELECT:

```
SELECT      *
FROM        tablename;
```

The above command would retrieve all columns and all rows from the named table.

The SELECT command and the FROM clause are necessary for

any SQL query. SELECT and FROM must appear before any other clauses in a query.

To retrieve only a specified set of rows from all columns of a table, state the common characteristic of the rows you want in a WHERE clause:

```
SELECT      *
FROM        tablename
WHERE       condition;
```

For example, to retrieve all of the information on the suppliers located in Dallas from the suppliers table, use the following command:

```
SELECT      *
FROM        suppliers
WHERE       city = 'Dallas';
```

You can specify any number of conditions to further delimit the set of rows you want to retrieve. For example, you may want to retrieve only those Dallas suppliers from whom you buy valves. You can do this by adding another condition to the WHERE clause:

```
SELECT      *
FROM        suppliers
WHERE       city = 'Dallas'
AND         part_name = 'valve';
```

There are many other possibilities for specifying the row or rows to be retrieved by adding terms to the WHERE clause. These are shown under various headings in Chapters 7, 8, and 9.

Rows returned in response to a SELECT command are retrieved and displayed in an arbitrary order. If you want them returned in a specific order, then you must use the term ORDER BY, which is discussed in Chapter 3.

5.5   The CREATE VIEW Command

Even though CREATE is a data definition command when used with CREATE TABLE and CREATE INDEX, the CREATE VIEW command is included in this list of data manipulation statements because it can only be completed by using the SELECT command.

You could set up a complicated query to select the information you want out of a large table, or you could create a view of the table showing only what you want. There are a number of advantages to creating a view. These and other special topics will be discussed in Chapter 9, which is devoted entirely to views.

The syntax for creating a view is:

```
CREATE VIEW viewname [(view_column_names)]
AS          SELECT   column1_name, column2_name, . . .
            FROM     tablename
            WHERE    condition;
```

The target list of view column names shown above after the viewname is optional. For example, if you wanted to see only those suppliers who supply filters, you could do so by creating a view of them, as follows:

```
CREATE VIEW filter_suppliers
AS          SELECT   name, address, part#, price
            FROM     suppliers
            WHERE    part_name = 'filters';
```

Note that the specification for the view is actually a SQL query. You may use any valid SQL query in a CREATE VIEW command, except that you cannot use an ORDER BY clause in a view. If you want the rows ordered in a specific way, you must do it with a separate query directed to the view after you have created it. The ordering of the rows retrieved from views is discussed in Chapter 9.

To query a view, use a WHERE clause just as you would use it in querying a table:

```
SELECT   column_name(s)
FROM     viewname
WHERE    condition(s);
```

If you change the information in the table underlying the view, the information in the view will also change. If you update the underlying table, the values in the view will also be updated. If you INSERT or DELETE rows in the table underlying the view, these rows will also be added to or deleted from the view. See Chapter 9 for further details on working with views.

Exercises

5.1. In Section 5.1 the statement appears ''If one column in a table contains a NOT NULL specification, then you cannot fill in any of the columns in that table until you have a value for the NOT NULL column.'' Is this statement simply a rule, or is there a logical reason behind it? If there is a logical reason, what is it?

5.2 Add a new employee named Carson, of Westville, SS # 32-4341, whose salary has not yet been determined, to the Employees table.

5.3 An employee named Gray has left the company. Remove his name from the Employee table and put it in a new table of Former Employees.

5.4 A table called Applicants was set up to hold the names and phone numbers of persons responding to a job opening. Since Carson was hired for this position, the other applicants' names are no longer needed. Remove this table from the database.

5.5 Query the database for the name, address, and SS# of all the accountants now employed.

5.6 Set up a virtual table containing all information on all accountants now employed.

5.7 Give all accountants a 5 percent raise.

5.8 Give all employees a 5 percent raise.

5.9 The New York supplier named Alcoe has now moved to Atlanta. Change this information in the database.

5.10 Set up a view showing salesmen's names and salaries.

Answers to Exercises

5.1 If you do not have a value for the NOT NULL column, then filling in any of the other columns in the table would leave the NOT NULL column blank, which is not allowed by NOT NULL specification.

5.2 INSERT
    INTO   employees
    VALUES   (' Carson', ' Westville', 32-4341, NULL);

5.3 CREATE TABLE former__employees
           (name   CHAR(10)
           SS#   NUM(8)
           title   CHAR(8));

    INSERT
    INTO   former__employees
             SELECT*
             FROM   employees
             WHERE name = ' Gray';

    DELETE
    FROM   employees
    WHERE   name = ' Gray';

5.4 DROP TABLE applicants;

5.5 SELECT name, address, SS#
    FROM   employees
    WHERE   title = ' accountants';

5.6 CREATE VIEW accountants
    AS   SELECT *
             FROM employees
             WHERE title = ' accountant';

5.7 UPDATE employees
    SET   salary = salary * 1.05
    WHERE   title = ' accountant';

5.8 UPDATE employees
    SET   salary = salary * 1.05;

5.9 UPDATE suppliers
    SET   city = ' Atlanta'
    WHERE   name = ' Alcoe';

5.10 CREATE VIEW salesmen
    AS   SELECT name, salary
                   FROM   employees
                   WHERE title = ' salesman';

6

Using the Data Control Statements

CERTAIN STATEMENTS PROVIDE A DATABASE ADMINISTRATOR (DBA) with the power to control access to the database and to institute procedures to preserve the integrity of the data. These considerations take on added significance in a multiuser system in which concurrent usage could lead to confusion among users and disruption of the system.

The SQL commands that exercise control over database access are GRANT and REVOKE. The basic SQL commands that preserve data integrity are COMMIT and ROLLBACK. Most commercial implementations also add constraints for auditing, locking, and index validation of the database.

6.1 Access Control

Even in single-user systems it may be necessary to control access to the database and to change access privileges from time to time. The GRANT and REVOKE commands provide a wide range of possibilities for access control.

6.1.1 The GRANT Command

The GRANT command can be used to allow either full access to the database or limited degrees of access. For example, as in some commercial systems now on the market, the type of access granted can be defined in terms of simply looking at database tables, looking at but not changing tables, looking only at views, looking at and changing views, or looking at all tables and views, making changes, and granting privileges to other users.

In this context, views combined with the access commands can safeguard specified columns in a table. To safeguard columns, set up a view of the table containing only those columns that are not confidential, while omitting the confidential columns from the view. Then grant access to the view rather than to the table itself. This procedure will be illustrated in the next section.

The syntax of the GRANT command is simply:

```
GRANT      specified_access ON tablename
TO         grantee_name, grantee_id;
```

where *grantee-name* is the name to be entered by the user who is being granted the privilege, whenever that user logs onto the system, and *grantee-id* is the password to be used by the privileged user in logging onto the system.

The *grantee-id* is not necessarily a part of SQL, but commercial versions of SQL usually require each user to have an individual id, or password, that must be used when entering the database. If that is the case, the system should be advised of the individual's password when the privilege(s) are granted as shown in the GRANT statement above.

Some types of access may carry the privilege of granting access to other users. For example, if tables in the database are identified with the name of the creator of the table, then that user (if he or she has been given the appropriate privilege) may GRANT access to his or her tables by other users. For example, the owner has given administrative assistant Baker access to all of the tables with the following command:

```
GRANT      ALL PRIVILEGES
TO         Baker

WITH GRANT OPTION;
```

He has now hired a secretary who does the billing under Baker's direction. Therefore the secretary, Ms. Doe, needs access to the Supplier table and the Customer table. The DBA gave Baker the right to grant access wherever necessary by adding WITH GRANT OPTION to his grant statement to her. Now Baker, in turn, can GRANT access to specific tables to Ms. Doe.

If Ms. Baker has created other tables or views—which she can do under the terms of her privileges—she has the inherent right to grant anyone else who has access to the database access to those tables or views that she created.

Ms. Baker may (because of the WITH GRANT OPTION stated in her own privileges) issue the following privileges to Ms. Doe:

```
GRANT     ALL PRIVILEGES ON suppliers, customers
TO        Doe;
```

With this command, Ms. Baker gives Ms. Doe the right to UPDATE, INSERT, and DELETE rows in the Suppliers Table and in the Customers Table. It also gives Ms. Doe the privilege of dropping both of these tables, creating indices on them, creating views on them, and using all of the data manipulation statements on the views. The GRANT statement does not give Ms. Doe the right to pass on her privileges to other users because the clause WITH GRANT OPTION was not included. If, however, Ms. Doe creates a view on either the Suppliers or the Customers tables, she can give other users the right to query that view and to make changes in it, since she "owns" the views she creates.

Granting Access to Specified Columns Only. Doe's use of the Suppliers and Customers tables involves using only the Part No. and Price columns; therefore Baker may wish to limit Doe's access to those columns. The command to do this is:

```
GRANT     ALL PRIVILEGES(Part#, Price) ON suppliers, customers
TO        Doe;
```

This command allows Doe to perform any data manipulation operation (SELECT, UPDATE INSERT, or DELETE) on the Suppliers and Customers tables, but only on the specified columns of those tables.

Granting Access to Several Specified Users at Once. If it is necessary for some personnel, but not all, to use certain tables and/or views, these users can all be named in one GRANT statement. For example, if the secretary (Doe) and the accountants (Walters and Riley) need access to the Suppliers table, then this can be handled with one GRANT statement, as follows:

```
GRANT     ALL PRIVILEGES ON Suppliers
TO        Doe, Walters, Riley;
```

PUBLIC Grantee. It might be convenient or necessary to make some tables or views available to everyone in the company. Rather than granting access (especially in a large company) to each individual by name, it is much more efficient for the dba to be able to do this with one command. This is the purpose of the grantee called PUBLIC. Any table or view to which PUBLIC is granted access is available to anyone in the organization possessing an id for entering the database.

PUBLIC access may be for reading the table only, not for changing it. If this is the case, then the GRANT statement would be:

```
GRANT SELECT ON          Suppliers
TO                       PUBLIC;
```

If, however, there is a possibility that someone may need to change the address of a supplier, then it should be possible for anyone to do so. This additional privilege can be granted by allowing UPDATE privileges to all, with the following statement:

```
GRANT UPDATE ON          Suppliers
TO                       PUBLIC;
```

If the list of customers is frequently being enlarged by the salesmen, then the opportunity to do so can be made available to them (as well as to everyone else) by the statement:

```
GRANT INSERT ON          Customers
TO                       PUBLIC;
```

The above command allows anyone who is authorized to use the database to add rows to the Customers table.

6.1.2   The REVOKE Command

Revoking access is simply the reverse of granting. It is accomplished by using the term REVOKE, naming the type of privilege previously granted, and then listing the name and id of the person whose access is being stopped. If different types of access have been granted, then by selectively revoking, either some or all of these levels can be revoked. The syntax is:

```
REVOKE      specified_privileges
FROM        username, userid;
```

For example, if at some later time, Ms. Baker leaves the company, the DBA will want to revoke all of her privileges. He can do this by using the command

```
REVOKE      ALL PRIVILEGES
FROM        Baker;
```

Depending upon how the user interface is set up, this may or may not leave in place the access(es) she has granted to other members of the firm.

6.1.3 Views as Security Devices

This topic is covered in Chapter 9, which is devoted to exclusively to views. In general, one of the prime reasons for using views rather than base tables is to restrict the use of certain parts of the table. Thus, views can be an important part of the security system of the database.

6.2 Integrity Control

The integrity controls COMMIT and ROLLBACK are contained in the ANSI Standard SQL Database Language and constitute the minimum controls necessary to maintain database integrity. Commercial multiuser systems employ additional controls, such as LOCK commands to prevent values from changing while a user is looking at or working with them. These LOCK commands sometimes include SHARED LOCK provisions so that several users may access tables at the same time without long waiting periods. Commercial multiuser systems may also incorporate into their SQL Data Control Statements various AUDIT commands, which provide a running record for the DBA as to which users are using which tables or views.

6.2.1 The COMMIT Command

The use of the COMMIT command allows user discretion as to when changes being made actually impinge upon the database. In this context, it is convenient to employ the concept of a *transaction* as discussed below.

Transactions. A transaction is a sequence of operations such that each operation in the sequence is necessary to complete a unitary result. In other words, if only part of the sequence were completed and entered into the database, then the database would be (or could be) in a state of imbalance or error. For example, if parts are sold and these parts are not removed from the inventory list, then the inventory list will show more parts than are actually on hand. Similarly, if, for example, a payment is made to a creditor's account, and the amount of this payment is not deducted from a bank balance, then the bank balance will be in error.

If a transaction requires that changes be made in several columns or in several tables, it may be that partial recording of that change will cause inconsistencies in the database. For example, entering the fact that an order has been filled may require (1) deducting the quantity and type of the part from inventory; (2) entering details of the shipment to the customer; (3) entering the amount now due from the customer; and (4) adding the amount due to income receivable by the user. Until all four of these items have been entered, the database will contain incompatible information.

Should a system breakdown occur in the course of such a sequence of entries, it may be time-consuming (or even impossible) to find the inconsistency and restore consistency to the database. For that reason, SQL provides the user with the option of committing changes to the database only when the transaction is complete. This is done with the command:

COMMIT WORK;

A transaction or part of a transaction that has not yet been COMMITted is visible only to the user entering it. It does not affect the database until the COMMIT statement is executed. Before the execution of the COMMIT statement, it can be *rolled back*, or eliminated (see the next section). After a transaction is COMMITted, it cannot be rolled back. If it has to be changed or corrected, that change must be done by means of another SQL statement such as UPDATE or DELETE.

A user interface may incorporate the automatic triggering of the COMMIT WORK command into selected operations on the database.

6.2.2 The ROLLBACK Command

If in the course of entering a transaction, an error is made, or if a transaction for some reason cannot (or should not, as for example, during a training session) be completed, the user may want to remove the changes in order to avoid inconsistencies in the database. The command ROLLBACK is supplied for this purpose.

For example, if a new employee was shown how to UPDATE, and the training process made partial changes in some tables, then the command to restore the database to its condition before the start of this transaction (i.e., to where it was after the last COMMIT statement) would be:

ROLLBACK WORK;

This command would remove any of the sequence of changes that were not followed by a COMMIT statement.

In the event of a system failure, database integrity can be preserved by an automatic ROLLBACK WORK feature that eliminates incomplete transactions and thus prevents their being entered into the database.

Exercises

The following exercises refer to a table called New Suppliers defined as follows:

```
CREATE TABLE new__suppliers
      (Name            CHAR(20)
      Address          CHAR(30)
      Phone            NUM(10)
      Part__Name       CHAR(12)
      Price            NUM(8)
      Terms            NUM(6)
      Rating           NUM(3));
```

Write SQL statements to do each of the following:

6.1   Give Martin SELECT privileges over the columns Name, Address, Phone, Part Name, and Price.

6.2   Give Smith UPDATE privileges over the entire table.

6.3   Give Fox full privileges over the entire table.

6.4   Give Brown SELECT privileges over the entire table.

6.5   Cancel all of Harro's privileges (assume he had ALL PRIVILEGEs) except SELECT on the entire table.

6.6   Remove all UPDATE privileges granted to users in exercises 6.1 through 6.5 above.

6.7 Remove all privileges from Martin.

6.8 Give Fox the right to give privileges he now holds to any other employees.

6.9 Give everyone in the organization the privilege of seeing the information in the New Suppliers Table.

6.10 Remove the privileges given in exercise 6.9 above.

Answers to Exercises

6.1 GRANT SELECT(name, address, phone, part__name, price)
ON new__suppliers
TO Martin;

6.2 GRANT UPDATE
ON new__suppliers
TO Smith;

6.3 GRANT ALL PRIVILEGES
ON new__suppliers
TO Fox;

6.4 GRANT SELECT
ON new__suppliers
TO Brown;

6.5 REVOKE UPDATE, INSERT, DELETE
ON new__suppliers
FROM Harro;

6.6 REVOKE UPDATE
ON new__suppliers
FROM Smith, Fox;

6.7 REVOKE SELECT
ON new__suppliers
FROM Martin;

6.8 GRANT SELECT, INSERT, DELETE
ON new__suppliers

```
      TO Fox
      WITH GRANT OPTION;

6.9   GRANT SELECT
      ON new__suppliers
      TO PUBLIC;

6.10  REVOKE SELECT
      ON new__suppliers
      FROM PUBLIC;
```

7

Logical Connectives, Aggregate Functions, and Subqueries

SQL IS DESIGNED TO MAKE USE OF THE BOOLEAN OPERATORS INTER-SECTION, UNION, and MINUS. Some versions of SQL now available present only the UNION operator, while making it possible, by the use of other terms, to achieve the results of an intersection operation and a minus term. Some present the INTERSECTION and UNION with no MINUS. Since a complete query language should be able to make use of all three Boolean operators directly, all are presented here.

This chapter will also discuss the use of the aggregate (or group) functions AVG, COUNT DISTINCT, COUNT(*), MAX, MIN, and SUM, and will illustrate the use of subqueries.

7.1 Logical Connectives

With SQL you can achieve all the results of the three operations of relational algebra, intersect, union, and minus. INTERSECTION is achieved by the use of AND. UNION is accomplished by using OR. Minus is achieved by using the word MINUS, and can be handled indirectly by using EXISTS and NOT EXISTS. MINUS can also be obtained by using IN and NOT IN. These logical connectives are illustrated in Sections 7.1.1 through 7.1.5 below.

7.1.1 The AND (Intersection) Connective

The AND in SQL has the same meaning and usage as the intersection of relational algebra. It is usually represented in SQL as AND, but some commercial systems refer to it as INTERSECTION. It is used to set up a query in which there are two conditions that must be met for the query to return one or more rows. Use the AND as follows:

```
SELECT     columns
FROM       tablename
WHERE      condition1
AND        condition2;
```

As an example using our fictional database, assume we want to find suppliers who sell parts with numbers higher than 12, and are located in Chicago. The query is set up as follows:

```
SELECT     supplier__name, part#
FROM       suppliers
WHERE      part# > '12'
AND        city = 'Chicago';
```

This will return only those rows that satisfy both condition 1 and condition 2. These are shown below:

Supplier Name	Part #
Best	15
Central	18

The above example uses the AND operator with two columns; it can also be used with more than two columns, and it can be used in conjunction with OR to form more complex queries. These uses will be exhibited in Section 7.1.3 after the use of OR has been illustrated.

7.1.2 The OR (Union) Connective

The Boolean union is represented in SQL by the term OR. It is the case where either one or both of two conditions are met.

Except for the substitution of the word OR for the AND, the SELECT statement will look exactly like that shown for the INTERSECTION, but the results may be very different depending on the contents of the database. The SQL query using the UNION will be:

```
SELECT      columns
FROM        tablename
WHERE       condition1
OR          condition2;
```

The rows returned will be those meeting either condition 1 or condition 2 or both. Note that when rows are returned that meet both condition 1 and condition 2, these are the same rows that would be returned by using AND. For example, using the same query as in Section 7.1.1 above but substituting OR for AND:

```
SELECT      supplier__name, part#, city
FROM        suppliers
WHERE city = 'Chicago'
OR          part# > 12;
```

will result in the following retrieval:

Supplier name	Part #	City
Acme	38	New York
Best	15	Chicago
Central	18	Chicago
Joe's	74	Wichita
Quiktool	22	Mobile

7.1.3   Using AND and OR in the Same Query

When using AND and OR in the same query, you should usually use parentheses to make the meaning clear. The placement of the parentheses can completely change the result. For example,

```
SELECT      supplier__name, part#
FROM        suppliers
WHERE       city = 'Dallas'
AND         part__name = 'valve'
AND         (part# = '15' OR part# = '74');
```

The above will return all Dallas suppliers of valves numbered 15 or 74. Contrast this with the following query:

```
SELECT        supplier__name, part#
FROM          suppliers
WHERE city  =  'Dallas'
AND           (part__name  =  'valve' AND part#  =  '15')
OR            part #  =  '74';
```

The above would return all Dallas suppliers of valves with part number 15, and all Dallas suppliers of parts numbered 74 whether or not these parts were valves. Therefore, the placement of the parentheses is important in making the meaning clear. In addition, ANSI assigns precedence values to connectives, with NOT having the highest precedence, followed in order by AND then OR. Also, implementors may assign precedence to the connectives that may or may not agree with the ANSI specifications. The only safe approach is to first know the precedence in your implementation, and then to use parentheses wherever possible to clarify your intent.

7.1.4 The MINUS (Difference) Operator

The MINUS operator can be used to retrieve rows that meet one condition while excluding another. It is set up to eliminate a condition rather than to add one. For example, if we wanted to find the suppliers of Part No. 30 who are not located in Chicago, we could set it up this way:

```
SELECT        supplier__name, part#, city
FROM          suppliers
WHERE         part#  =  '30'
MINUS
SELECT        supplier__name, part#, city
FROM          suppliers
WHERE city  =  'Chicago';
```

The datatypes and their widths in the above two SELECT statements must match. The result is only the rows retrieved by the first SELECT that do not match those retrieved by the second SELECT.

The same result can be obtained by using NOT. For example, to find the suppliers of Part No. 30 who are not located in Chicago, you could enter:

```
SELECT      supplier__name, part#, city
FROM        suppliers
WHERE       NOT city  =  'Chicago'
AND         part#  =  '30';
```

which would give the same result as the query above using MINUS. You could also write the WHERE clause:

```
WHERE       city < > 'Chicago';
```

But you cannot use:

```
WHERE       city NOT  =  'Chicago';
```

7.1.5 Substituting IN and NOT IN for AND, OR, or MINUS

The IN and NOT IN connectives are used to test for membership in a class or to exclude members of a specified class. Obviously, it is sometimes possible to use these interchangeably with the AND, OR, or MINUS connectives.

One procedure is to list the class members and specify whether the result is to be IN or NOT IN that list, as follows:

```
SELECT      supplier__name, part#, city
FROM        suppliers
WHERE       city IN ('New__York', 'Atlanta', 'Boston');
```

The above command will retrieve the specified columns for all suppliers in the three cities named. This is the same result we would get if we worded the command as follows:

```
SELECT      supplier__name, part#, city
FROM        suppliers
WHERE       city  =  'New__York'
OR          city  =  'Atlanta'
OR          city  =  'Boston';
```

Clearly, the command using IN is much simpler and shorter than the one using OR.

The connective NOT IN will exclude the values within the parentheses. For example, the query shown above under Section 7.1.4, "Find the suppliers of Part No. 30 who are not located in Chicago," could be set up as follows:

```
SELECT      supplier__name, part#, city
FROM        suppliers
WHERE       part#  =  ' 30'
AND         city NOT IN (' Chicago');
```

The result above is the same as it would be if we entered:

```
SELECT      supplier__name, part#, city
FROM        suppliers
WHERE       part#  =  ' 30'
MINUS
SELECT      supplier__name, part#, city
FROM        suppliers
WHERE       city  =  ' Chicago';
```

It could also be entered as:

```
WHERE       part#  =  ' 30'
AND         NOT (city  =  ' Chicago');
```

But it cannot be entered as:

```
WHERE       part#  =  ' 30'
AND         city NOT  =  ' Chicago';
```

In general, when you are using NOT to exclude a condition (i.e., in place of the word "except"), enclose the set to be excluded in parentheses, and precede the set with NOT. This form is necessary because SQL arose out of the predicate calculus, in which the equal sign (=) and the quantities before and after it constitute a predicate, and although NOT can modify a predicate, it cannot be a part of a predicate.

Other uses of the NOT connective are shown in Section 3.2.2 of Chapter 3 with the BETWEEN predicate, and in Section 3.2.4 Chapter 3 with LIKE.

7.2   The Aggregate Functions

The aggregate functions, also called *group* or *built-in* functions in some implementations, supported by SQL are average (AVG), count (COUNT DISTINCT), count (COUNT*), maximum (MAX), minimum (MIN), and SUM. In each case, the aggregate functions return a single value as a summary of information about a group of rows in a column.

The aggregate function is placed in the SELECT command. The result is displayed in the form of a table with a single column with one row. This is illustrated below.

Aggregate functions can appear in the main query or in a subquery. They may also be used in conjunction with comparison operators and value expressions.

If an aggregate function is applied to one of the columns selected, then an aggregate function (not necessarily the same aggregate function) must be applied to all other columns selected. In other words, you cannot mix a query for individual values with one for aggregate values in the same SELECT statement—unless the query contains a GROUP BY clause. In other words, you can include an individual value column in the SELECT only if you are GROUPing on that column. For example, the following query is not legal:

```
SELECT      title, AVG(salary)
FROM        employees;
```

But this one is legal:

```
SELECT      title, AVG(salary)
FROM        employees
GROUP BY    title;
```

Note that NULL values are treated differently by different aggregate functions; the precise treatment given to NULLs is noted under the specific section applying to each aggregate function.

You can use more than one aggregate function in a SELECT statement. Below we have constructed a rather unlikely query combining all six functions:

```
SELECT      AVG(salary), MIN(salary), MAX(salary), SUM(salary),
                COUNT DISTINCT, COUNT(*)
FROM        employees;
```

The above command will return the average, minimum, and maximum salary, the total of all salaries, the number of different salaries (eliminating NULLs and duplicates), and the number of salaries listed (which will be the same as the number of employees).

NULL values in a column are eliminated before any of the above aggregate functions are computed—except for COUNT(*), which handles NULL values just like non-NULL values. In other words, COUNT(*) will return the number of entries in the designated column regardless of whether they are duplicates, NULL values, or other values. COUNT DISTINCT will count the number of different values in the column and will not include NULLs in the total.

The term DISTINCT is used to eliminate duplicate values in a column. It is usually used with aggregate functions and is optional with SUM and AVG, meaningless with MAX and MIN, and mandatory with COUNT. If you want COUNT to include any duplication that may be in the columns, then this must be indicated by using the function COUNT (*).

7.2.1 The AVERAGE (AVG) Operator

If AVG is specified, then the datatype of the result cannot be a character string. Also, if AVG is specified and the values in the designated column are exact numeric, then the datatype of the result is exact numeric with user-defined precision and scale. For example, to find the average salary of all employees of the company, enter:

```
SELECT      AVG(Salary)
FROM        Employees;
```

The result will be a table with one column and one row, such as:

AVG(salary)

3025.45

You could also find the average of a specified group or a number of groups with one command. For example, if you wanted to find the average salary of accountants, enter:

```
SELECT      AVG(salary)
FROM        employees
WHERE       title  =  ' accountant';
```

If you want to find the average of each of several types of classifications within a column, you could enter several individual queries to do so, but it would be more efficient to do it with one query using both the AVG function and the GROUP BY clause. For example, you could find the average salary of many different job classifications by entering:

```
SELECT      AVG(salary)
FROM        employees
GROUP BY    title;
```

The result would be in the following form:

Title	AVG(salary)
Secretary	900
Accountant	1500
Salesman	2000
Programmer	1200

NULL values are ignored by the AVG function. This may sometimes be confusing since the value returned may not be the sum of the column values divided by the number of values in the column. Instead, the AVG function will divide by the number of non-NULL values in the column.

7.2.2 The COUNT Function

The COUNT function must be followed by the specification DISTINCT. This eliminates duplicate rows. (Note that the same is not true of the COUNT(*)function.) Specifically, the NULL values are eliminated before the function is applied.

Unlike the other aggregate functions, if the argument specified is an empty set, COUNT will return a value of zero. (The other functions will return null.)

COUNT returns the number of values in the column. The mandatory DISTINCT ensures that no duplicates have been counted. For example, if we needed to know how many suppliers we now make use of, we would enter:

```
SELECT      COUNT (DISTINCT supplier__name)
FROM        suppliers;
```

The result will be a number indicating the number of different supplier names ocurring in the Supplier Name column of the Suppliers table.

7.2.3 Using COUNT(*)

In contrast to COUNT(DISTINCT), if we were to query the Suppliers table with COUNT(*), it would list the total number of supplier names in the table disregarding the fact that some suppliers may be listed more than once. In that case, we would obtain a different result by using COUNT(*) than we would by using COUNT(DISTINCT).

7.2.4 The SUM Function

The SUM function adds the values in the specified column and returns a single value. The column must contain numeric values. NULL values are eliminated, and therefore do not affect the value returned.

The SUM function may be used, for example, to find the total company expenditure for salaries:

```
SELECT      SUM(salary)
FROM        employees;
```

7.2.5 MAX and MIN

The MAX function returns the largest value in a column; the MIN function returns the smallest value in a column. The specification DISTINCT is meaningless with these two functions and should not be used.

We could determine the highest-priced part listed by the suppliers in our Suppliers table by entering:

```
SELECT      MAX(price)
FROM        Suppliers;
```

Since the above query would only tell us the price and not the name of the part, however, we would be more likely to use a subquery to answer the question. (Subqueries are discussed in detail in Section 7.4.) It would appear as:

```
SELECT      part__name, price
FROM        suppliers
WHERE       price  =
```

```
(SELECT        MAX(price)
 FROM          suppliers);
```

7.3   Aliases

While aliases have many potential uses, the principal uses of substitute names for tables and columns are the following:

1. To make a cryptic column name more meaningful when it is displayed.

2. To abbreviate an often-used table or column name.

3. To make a complicated SQL statement clearer.

4. To distinguish between two appearances of the same column-name or table-name in any one SELECT statement.

In addition, table and column aliases may be used whenever it is convenient to do so.

The purpose listed above as item four usually involves a join of a table with itself, and therefore is considered in Chapter 8, which is devoted exclusively to joins.

7.3.1   Column Aliases

To create a column alias, enter the alias after the column name in the SELECT statement. For example, to make the computed column AVG(SAL) more meaningful when displayed (e.g., in a report), enter:

```
SELECT       title, AVG(SAL) 'Average Salary'
FROM         employees
GROUP BY     title
HAVING       AVG(SAL) >
             (SELECT AVG(SAL)
             FROM   employees
             WHERE  title < > 'secretary');
```

The above query will list the AVG(SAL) of all employee titles for which that average is greater than the average for secretaries, and the column heading will be "Average Salary" rather than AVG(SAL). Note that the column alias is only referred to in the SELECT statement. It is enclosed in single quotes because it consists of two words that are to be shown together over the displayed results. If the column alias were a single word (and contained no special characters such as *, &, or %, the single quotes would not be necessary.

7.3.2 Table Aliases

To create a table alias, define it in the FROM clause. The alias is then used as a qualifier in both the SELECT and WHERE clauses. For example, if you want to abbreviate the table name Salesmen to S, and the Customer table to C, in order to combine certain salesmen with customers, enter:

```
SELECT     S.*, C.*
FROM       salesmen S, customers C
WHERE      S.district = C.district;
AND        S.commission > 3000;
```

The use of the qualifying S. in the AND clause is not absolutely necessary, since only the Salesmen table contains a commission; however, it is never wrong to use the complete specification whether or not an alias is being used.

7.4 Subqueries

A subquery specifies a set of values derived from the result of a FROM, WHERE, HAVING, or GROUP BY clause. It is a query contained in the WHERE clause that will provide you with the results you need to complete the main query. In some database systems, subqueries are called *nested SELECTs*.

Subqueries are useful in building powerful, complex queries. They can always be broken down into two or more simple queries, but in most cases it is more efficient to use the subquery than the collection of simple queries. There is no limit in SQL on the number of subqueries that can be nested, but there may be a limit in the user interface. Such expressions, however, may become so complex that the use of a set of queries with fewer subqueries may be advisable.

A general syntax for a query containing a subquery is:

```
SELECT     column1, column2, . . ., columnN
FROM       tablename1
WHERE      column_i IN
                (SELECT     column_j
                 FROM       tablename2
                 WHERE      condition);
```

where *column_i* and *column_j* have the same datatype and width.

The subquery, or *inner query*, starts with the second SELECT, and is always surrounded by parentheses. The query starting with the first SELECT is called the *main query* or the *outer query*.

Theoretically, another subquery can be added after the second WHERE clause, and that same process repeated again and again. In practice, however, too many subqueries can become confusing.

A subquery can refer to a table other than the one referred to by the main query, and you can use comparison operators other than IN to connect the query with the subquery.

You can use a subquery wherever you can use a WHERE clause (i.e., in SELECT, UPDATE, INSERT, and DELETE commands). You can use GROUP BY and HAVING clauses, but you cannot use OR-DER BY or UNION clauses in a subquery. As an example of a subquery from our fictional database, suppose you want to list all salesmen whose commission is greater than $800. You can do so with the following command:

```
SELECT      employee__name, title, commission
FROM        employees
WHERE       employee__name IN
            (SELECT    employee__name
            FROM       employees
            WHERE      commission > 800
            AND        title = ' salesman');
```

You could use the equal sign (=) in the first WHERE clause above and omit the IN, if you know ahead of time that only one row will be returned, as follows:

```
WHERE       employees =
            (SELECT    employee__name
            FROM       employees
            WHERE      commission > 800
            AND        title = ' salesman');
```

If more than one row satisfies the subquery when the equal sign (=) is used, then SQL will return an error. If no rows satisfy the subquery and the equal sign (=) is used in the first WHERE clause, then SQL will return a NULL. Obviously, if you don't know how many rows will be returned, it is safer to use IN than the equal sign (=).

You can also use a subquery to SELECT more than one column. In this case, put parentheses around the list of columns on the left side of the comparison operator. For example if we want to find the suppliers who sell the same part at the same price as Acme, we would enter:

```
SELECT      supplier__name, part__name, price
FROM        suppliers
WHERE       (part__name, price) IN
            (SELECT      part__name, price
            FROM        suppliers
            WHERE       supplier__name = 'Acme');
```

You can combine a number of conditions in the WHERE clause by using AND and OR to connect these conditions in the subqueries. You may also use a subquery composed of two or more queries by using the operators AND, OR, and MINUS. These operators are useful when you construct subqueries referring to different tables. The use of subqueries with the connectors mentioned in this paragraph is illustrated in the sections devoted specifically to those connectors.)

You can use a subquery with EXISTS to test for existence. For example, for the query: "List all customers for which there is a supplier in the same city," enter:

```
SELECT      customer__name
FROM        customers
WHERE       EXISTS
      (SELECT city
      FROM suppliers
      WHERE   supplier.city = customer.city);
```

The above query will return a list of all customers in a city where there is a supplier.

Exercises

Use the following tables to complete the exercises listed below:

Courses

Course Name	Credit Hours	Semester	Staff
Geography	3	Fall	Blane
Architecture	5	Summer	Smith

Course Name	Credit Hours	Semester	Staff
Trigonometry	3	Spring	Weeks
Planning	2	Spring	Jones
Psychology	3	Fall	Martin
Psychology	3	Spring	Gerber
Psychology	3	Fall	Gerber
Psychology	3	Spring	Martin
Biology	4	Fall	Gregory
Biology	4	Spring	Allen
Astronomy	5	Spring	Barnes
Biology	3	Summer	Allen
Algebra	2	Summer	Blane
Algebra	3	Fall	Weeks

Faculty

Name	Rank
Smith	Instructor
Gerber	Assistant Prof.
Weeks	Assistant Prof.
Allen	Instructor
Barnes	Professor
Blane	Instructor
Gregory	Assistant Prof.
Jones	Assistant Prof.
Martin	Assistant Prof.

Write the SQL statements for the following queries:

7.1 List the courses and credit hours of courses taught by Barnes in the spring semester.

7.2 List the courses either taught by Barnes or offered in the spring semester.

7.3 List the courses either taught by Barnes in the fall, or taught by Martin in the fall.

7.4 Find the number of different instructors and the number of different ranks.

7.5   Determine the average number of credit hours taught by instructors.

7.6. Find all courses of four semester hours or less, taught in the spring semester by an assistant professor.

7.7   Find all courses of at least three semester hours taught by someone other than Smith.

7.8   List the fall courses and the faculty who teach them, with the faculty names shown alphabetically.

7.9   Determine the number of courses covered by the course list, and the number of different faculty members teaching.

7.10 List the fall or spring courses that are taught by assistant professors.

Answers to Exercises

7.1	SELECT	course__name, credit__hours
	FROM	courses
	WHERE	staff = ' Barnes'
	AND	semester = ' spring';

7.2	SELECT$	course__name
	FROM	courses
	WHERE	staff = ' Barnes'
	OR	semester = ' spring';

7.3	SELECT	course__name
	FROM	courses
	WHERE	(staff = ' Barnes' OR staff = ' Martin')
	AND	semester = ' fall';

It could also be entered as:

	SELECT	course__name
	FROM	courses
	WHERE	staff = ' Barnes'
	AND	semester = ' fall'
	UNION	

```
        SELECT      course__name
        FROM        courses
        WHERE       staff  =  ' Martin'
        AND         semester  =  ' fall';
```

7.4   SELECT COUNT (DISTINCT instructors), COUNT (DISTINCT ranks)
        FROM   faculty;

7.5   SELECT   AVG(credit__hours)
        FROM   courses
        WHERE   staff IN
                    (SELECT   name
                     FROM   faculty
                     WHERE   rank = ' instructor');

7.6   SELECT   course__name
        FROM   courses
        WHERE   credit__hours < = 4
        AND   staff IN
                    (SELECT   name
                     FROM   faculty
                     WHERE   rank = ' assist__prof');

7.7   SELECT course__name
        FROM   courses
        WHERE   NOT staff = ' Smith'
        AND   credit__hours > = 3;

7.8   SELECT   course__name, staff
        FROM   courses
        WHERE   semester = ' fall'
        ORDER BY   staff;

7.9   SELECT COUNT(*), COUNT (DISTINCT staff)
        FROM   courses;

7.10   SELECT course__name,
        FROM courses
        WHERE (semester = spring OR semester = fall)
        AND   staff IN
                    (SELECT   staff
                     FROM   faculty
                     WHERE   rank = ' assist__prof');
```
```

8

Joins

THE ABILITY TO FORM JOINS IS PROBABLY ONE OF SQL'S MOST POWER-ful characteristics. It is also one of the most important features distinguishing a relational database from other types of database systems. Forming joins is, therefore, a rather highly developed aspect of the SQL language.

A *join* in SQL is a query in which data are retrieved from two or more tables (or views). The purpose of joining is to retrieve information that is not in any single table or view. (For convenience we will refer here only to tables being joined, but it should be understood that the objects being joined could be views.)

This chapter will explore and illustrate equijoins, non-equijoins, natural joins, outer joins, joining more than two tables, joining a table with itself, joining tables to views, and joining views to views.

8.1 Equijoins

The equijoin in SQL is represented by:

```
SELECT     table1.*, table2. *
FROM       table1, table2
WHERE      (set of conditions);
```

where (set of conditions) is a collection of equality comparisons between columns of Table 1 and columns of Table 2. The columns compared must be of the same type and width.

8.1.1 The Cartesian Product

If the set of conditions in the equijoin shown in Section 8.1 is empty, then the result is the Cartesian product. In other words, if you juxtapose each row of Table 1 with each row of Table 2, (without eliminating any rows of either table), then the result is the Cartesian product of Table 1 and Table 2. In this case, there is no need for a WHERE clause. Therefore, the command for doing this is:

```
SELECT      *
FROM        table1, table2;
```

For example, consider Table 1, containing columns A, B, and C, and Table 2 containing columns C, D, and E below:

Table 1				Table 2		
A	B	C		C	D	E
1	1	1		1	4	5
1	2	1		2	6	7
2	2	1		3	8	9
1	2	2				

The Cartesian product of Tables 1 and 2 (which is an equijoin of Tables 1 and 2) is Table 3 below containing columns A, B, C, C, D, and E:

Table 3

T_1A	T_1B	T_1C	T_2C	T_2D	T_2E
1	1	1	1	4	5
1	1	1	2	6	7
1	1	1	3	8	9
1	2	1	1	4	5
1	2	1	2	6	7
1	2	1	3	8	9
2	2	1	1	4	5
2	2	1	2	6	7

T_1A	T_1B	T_1C	T_2C	T_2D	T_2E
2	2	1	3	8	9
1	2	2	1	4	5
1	2	2	2	6	7
1	2	2	3	8	9

If the two tables being joined contain two (or more) column names that are the same, then these are called *common columns*. Column T_1C and T_2C in the above example are such common columns.

8.1.2 Equijoin with One Condition

If the set of conditions consists of only one comparison, then we have:

```
SELECT      table1.*, table2. *
FROM        table1, table2
WHERE       (condition);
```

where the comparison operator in the (condition) is an equals (=) sign.

Usually you will want to obtain an equijoin when two tables have a common column, and the *set of conditions* in the WHERE clause specifies that the values in the common columns are equal. The common column is called the *join column*. The syntax for doing this is:

```
SELECT      table1.*, table2. *
FROM        table1, table2
WHERE       table1.join_column = table2.join_column;
```

Note that in this case, it is necessary to use the table name identification with each of the join columns to make it clear that they come from different tables. The results are shown in Table 4 below:

Table 4

T_1A	T_1B	T_1C	T_2C	T_2D	T_2E
1	1	1	1	4	5
1	2	1	1	4	5
2	2	1	1	4	5
1	2	2	2	6	7

8.1.3   The Natural Join

The natural join, which is usually referred to simply as a *join*, is obtained by taking an equijoin on the common column of two tables and then removing the duplicate of the common column. This results in:

Table 5

A	B	C	D	E
1	1	1	4	5
1	2	1	4	5
2	2	1	4	5
1	2	2	6	7

which is Table 4 from Section 8.1.2 above with the duplicate "C" column eliminated.

In SQL, you can obtain the natural join of Tables 1 and 2 by entering:

```
SELECT      table1.*, D, E,
FROM        table1, table2
WHERE       table1.join_column = table2.join_column;
```

It is not necessary to use the table name identification for columns D and E in the SELECT statement because those columns only appear in Table 2 above.

8.1.4   Join on Specified Columns Only

If you do not want to display all of the columns that appear in the natural join, then you can form a join of specified columns by listing the columns you want after the SELECT:

```
SELECT      table1.columns, table2.columns
FROM        table1, table2
WHERE       join_column1 = join_column2;
```

The above means that the retrieval will consist of the columns you want displayed from Table 1 and Table 2 wherever the row value in the join column in Table 1 is the same as the row value in the join column in Table 2.

As an example, suppose we wanted to assign customers to salesmen who live in the same district as the customer. Given that we have a Salesmen table listing only salesmen and their districts, and a Customer table showing only customers and their districts, we would then join the Salesmen table to the Customer table wherever the salesman's district matched the customer's district, as follows:

```
SELECT      salesmen.*, customers.*
FROM        salesmen, customers
WHERE       salesmen.district = customer.district
GROUP BY    district;
```

Note that the column names in the WHERE clause are qualified by preceding them with the table name. This is because these columns have the same name in each of the tables, and the column name alone is ambiguous. (Note that join columns do not have to have the same name.)

The equijoin will retrieve the columns requested, and among these will be two identical columns (i.e., join_column1 and join_column2—District in both cases). The results will look like the following:

Salesman name	District	Customer name	District
Fox	Southpark	Minton	Southpark
Fox	Southpark	Winters	Southpark
Fox	Southpark	Summers	Southpark
Smith	Northpark	Barnes	Northpark
Smith	Northpark	Gaylord	Northpark
Harro	Westerly	Carter	Westerly
Baker	Eastern	Sutton	Eastern
Baker	Eastern	Wiley	Eastern

To obtain this join without the duplicate column, SELECT all columns from either table and then SELECT only the necessary column in the other table, leaving out the column that would be a duplicate. In the query below, we have Selected all from the Salesmen table and only the name from the Customer table:

```
SELECT      salesmen.*, customers.name
FROM        salesmen, customers
WHERE       salesmen.district = customers.district
GROUP BY    district;
```

The result will show only one District column.

8.2 Non-Equijoins

If we want to join columns in two tables in which the join column in one table is not equal to the corresponding join column in the other table, this is called a *non-equijoin*. The general syntax for a non-equijoin is:

```
SELECT      table1.columns, table2.columns
FROM        table1, table2
WHERE       join_column1
            (any comparison operator except = ) join column2
```

where the comparison operator may be: greater than (>), less than (<), not equal to (< >).

As an example, instead of assigning salesmen to customers in the same districts as those in which the salesmen live, you could do it the other way: assign salesmen to customers who do not live in their home districts. To do this, enter:

```
SELECT      salesmen.*, customers.*
FROM        salesmen, customers
WHERE       NOT salesmen.districts = customers.districts;
```

Or, the WHERE clause could be entered as:

```
WHERE       salesmen.districts < > customers.districts;
```

The resulting display would match salesmen with customers unpredictably, except for the fact that there would be no rows in which the saleman's district was the same as the customer's district. (Note that in the above query, the NOT must come before the search condition as shown. The expression

```
WHERE salesmen.districts NOT = customer.district
```

is not a legal form of the predicate.)

8.3 Additional Conditions in Join Queries

The WHERE clause in a join query may be used to specify any number of conditions. To do so, use an AND to specify the additional condition(s). If the salesmen discussed in the preceding sections were actually listed in a table containing all employees, then we would want to qualify the query so that the secretary, the accountant, and the programmers would not be linked with customers. Another condition in the join query will accomplish this. Enter:

```
SELECT      employee.name, customer.name
FROM        employees, customers
WHERE       employee.district = customer.district
AND         employee.title = ' salesman';
```

This query will join salesmen with customers according to matching districts, without matching any nonsales personnel with customers.

Any number of conditions may be added to the WHERE clause by the use of the AND operator.

8.4 Joining More than Two Tables

Any number of tables can be joined. This is accomplished by naming the tables to be joined in the FROM clause and using the AND to add any conditions necessary.

```
SELECT      column_names
FROM        table1, table2, . . . tableN
WHERE       (condition1)
AND         (condition2)
. . .
AND         (conditionM);
```

There is no theoretical limit on the number of joins possible, although the implementor may impose a limit.

8.5 Joining Tables to Views

You can join a table and a view (or more than one of each) in the same way you join a table to a table. For example, if you want to join an entire view to certain columns of a table, you would use the following:

```
SELECT    viewname.*, tablename.column1, tablename.column2,
          . . . tablename.columnN
FROM      viewname, tablename;
```

8.6 Creating a View from a Join

The two operations of creating a view and forming a join from two or more tables can be accomplished simultaneously by adding the SELECT statement as a subquery specifying the join commands to the CREATE VIEW statement, as follows:

CREATE VIEW viewname (column_name,
            column_name . . .)
    AS   (subquery)

where (*subquery*) is defined as:

(SELECT *table1_column, table2_column*
 FROM *table1, table2*
 WHERE *join_column1 (comparison operator) join_column2*);

If we wanted to join just the salesmen's names and districts with the customer names and districts in the example in Section 8.3 above (where salesmen are listed in the Employees table), we could create a view called Assignments instead of using both of the entire tables. To do so, enter:

```
CREATE VIEW       assignments
AS   (SELECT      employee.name, employee.district, customer.name,
                     customer.district
FROM              employees,  customers
     WHERE        employee.district = customer.district
     AND          title = ' salesman'
     GROUP BY     district;
```

This would yield the view called Assignments, showing only the salesmen's names and districts, linked with the customer's names and districts. The resulting display would be exactly the same as that shown in Section 8.1.4.

8.7 Joining Views to Views

Views can be joined to views in the same way that tables are joined to tables. The names of the views being joined should appear after the FROM, just as tables being joined are named in the FROM clause.

8.8 Joining a Table with Itself

It may sometimes be desirable to join rows in the same table. Aliases can be used to advantage in this situation. For example, you might want a list of pairs of salesmen who are in the same city.

To do this, you must list the table twice in the FROM clause, and then distinguish the two listings by giving each an alias. For the query: "List all pairs of salesmen who are in the same city," enter:

```
SELECT    First.name, Second.name
FROM      Salesmen First, Salesmen Second
WHERE     First.City = Second.City
AND       First.SS# > Second.SS#;
```

The FROM clause assigns the alias "First" to the Salesmen Table, and the alias "Second" to the same Salesmen Table. The specification after the AND, which indicates that the first SS# must be greater than the second, prevents the result from showing a salesman paired with himself (Jones, Jones), and prevents it from giving us the same pairing twice, as for example (Jones, Smith) and (Smith, Jones).

For some queries, there are other ways to combine a table with itself, but the use of aliases often makes the meaning clearer.

8.9 Outer Joins

In some situations it may be useful to retrieve rows that meet one of the join conditions, but not both. Such cases are called *outer joins*.

Outer joins are important because they may retrieve data that might otherwise be lost if the join condition alone is used for retrieval. For example, a join column may contain rows that would fit the join condition except that they have NULL values in the second join column. It may be that if those NULL values were filled in with non-NULL values, the join condition would be completely satisfied. With the join retrieval, these rows would not be picked up. An outer join retrieval would return these rows; they can then be examined to determine whether or not supplying the missing values would satisfy the join condition.

It may be helpful in conceptualizing outer joins to realize that joins are analogous to the *Intersection* of sets (the join includes all rows that are members of both sets) and outer joins are analogous to the (exclusive) *union* of sets (the outer join includes rows that are members of one but not both of the specified sets).

Outer joins are not supported directly by the SQL language, although Codd referred to them and set forth the requirements for an outer join syntax [21]. Some commercial databases that use SQL, notably *ORACLE*, do offer support for outer joins. This is accomplished by the use of an outer-join operator, which is a plus (+) sign in *ORACLE*'s copyrighted interface to SQL called *SQL*Plus [51]*. (Also see references *[11]* and *[27]* on this topic.)

The query used by *ORACLE* to retrieve the outer join is set up this way:

```
SELECT      table1.columns, table2.columns
FROM        table1, table2
WHERE       join_column1 = join_column2 (+);
```

The outer join symbol, plus (+), tells *SQL*Plus* to treat Table 1 as if it contained an extra row with a NULL value in every column; the interface then joins this NULL row of Table 1 to any row of Table 2 that cannot be joined to an existing row of Table 1. In this way, *ORACLE* picks up the outer join by combining SQL commands with a special outer join command built into the interface.

An example of the need to retrieve an outer join can be illustrated in our matching of salesmen's districts with customers' districts. If there happened to be a customer in a district where no salesman lived, there would be no match with this customer. Therefore, there would be no salesman servicing that customer. Conversely, if there were a salesman who lived in a district where there were no customers, this salesman would not be matched with any customer.

Exercises

Use the following tables to complete the exercises below:

Candidates

Name	District	Office
Smith	7	Council
Breag	3	Council
Jones	3	Mayor
Sherman	6	Council
Olson	6	Coroner
Wilson	4	Council
Black	1	Sheriff
Fortin	2	D.A.
Leery	2	Council

Volunteers

Name	District
Deeds	1
Burk	1
Lyman	2
Merrik	2
Martinez	2
Volnik	3
Stacio	4
Rudd	11

Write SQL statements for exercises 8.1 through 8.3 below:

8.1 For the Cartesian product of Candidates and Volunteers.

8.2 For the natural join of Candidates and Volunteers.

8.3 List the Candidates with the Volunteers who are in the same District.

8.4 Consider the following Relay Runner database table:

Runner	Lap	Team
Jones	1	Golden Angels
Richards	2	Golden Angels
Ignatz	3	Golden Angels
Camp	4	Golden Angels
Williams	1	East
Agronsky	2	East
Stevens	3	East
Smith	4	East

Form the self join of this table that will give the name of each runner in the same row with the name of the runner to whom he hands the baton.

8.5 Let the Coaches table in the same database be:

Runner	Coach
Jones	Wesson
Richards	Caps
Ignatz	Wesson
Camp	Caps
Williams	East

Runner	Coach
Agronsky	Johanson
Stevens	Johanson
Smith	Mickey

Find which team each coach works for.

8.6 Find those coaches whose names are the same as the name of the team they work for.

8.7 Let the Owners table be:

Owner	Team
Millions	Golden Angels
Scrooge	East

Find the runners and the owners they work for.

8.8 Find the runners, coaches, and owners that are with the same team.

8.9 Let the Team City table be:

Team	City
Golden Angels	Dallas
East	New York

Find the Owners and the City their team is in.

8.10 Find the runners, coaches, and owners that are with the same team, and the city they are in.

Answers to Exercises

8.1 SELECT   candidates.*, volunteers.*
     FROM   candidates, volunteers;

8.2 SELECT   candidates.*, volunteers.name
     FROM   candidates, volunteers
     WHERE   candidates.district = volunteers.district
     AND   candidates.name = volunteers.name;

8.3 SELECT   candidates.*, volunteers.*
     FROM   candidates, volunteers
     WHERE   candidates.district = volunteers.district;

8.4 SELECT   First.*, Second.*

```
           FROM         relay__runners
           WHERE        First.lap = Second.lap − 1
           AND          First.Team = Second.Team;


8.5        SELECT       Team, Coach
           FROM         Relay__runners,Coaches
           WHERE        Relay__runners.runner = Coaches.runner;


8.6        SELECT       Team,Coach
           FROM         Relay__runners,Coaches
           WHERE        Relay__runners.runner = Coaches.runner
           AND          Team = Coach;


8.7        SELECT       Runner,Owner
           FROM         Relay__runners,Owners
           WHERE        Relay__runners.Team = Owners.Team;


8.8        SELECT       runner,Coach,Owner
           FROM         Relay__runners,Coaches,Owners
           WHERE        Relay__runners.Team = Owners.Team
           AND          Relay__runners.runner = Coaches.runner;


8.9        SELECT       Owner,City
           FROM         Owners,Team__city
           WHERE        Owners.Team = Team__city.Team;


8.10       SELECT       Runner,Coach,Owner,City
           FROM         Relay__runners,Coaches,Owners,Team__city
           WHERE        Relay__runners.Team = Owners.Team
           AND          Relay__runners.runner = Coaches.runner
           AND          Owners.Team = Team__city.Team;
```

9

Working with Views, Indices, and Queries

WHILE VIEWS HAVE ALREADY BEEN ENCOUNTERED EARLIER IN THIS text, the convenience and security they offer make it necessary to consider them in greater detail. Therefore, the early part of this chapter illustrates views in detail.

Queries and indices are discussed further in this chapter because SQL commands specify only what information is wanted, not how to get it out of the database. Most complete relational database systems include an implementor-supplied facility for optimizing the access paths to the data being sought; however, proper design, based on an understanding of relational theory, can contribute to high performance. Also, the end user who becomes thoroughly familiar with SQL can enhance the optimization process in two ways:

- By creating sufficient and appropriate indices
- By constructing queries to take advantage of the system

These two optimization processes are somewhat complementary because an understanding of the purpose and function of indices will lead to the optimal construction of queries.

This chapter will discuss indices in detail and will also cover the performance advantages inherent in the wording of certain SQL statements.

9.1 Views

There are three main purposes for working with views:

- As a database grows large, it is usually much more convenient to work with a view consisting of selected columns from a table rather than the whole table. A simple query to a view containing only those columns you intend to work with in a given session can be far easier to construct than a query selecting a few specific columns out of a large table.

- Tables may contain more information than should prudently be displayed to all employees who might use the database (such as salaries, or specifications for new products). If this is the case with a specific table, then use of the table itself may be restricted to a few specified employees, while the nonconfidential columns are set up as a view and made available to all who work with the database.

- In large, multiuser systems, views can provide the means for different users to see the same data in different ways and, depending on the capacity of the system, possibly at the same time.

Therefore, views often provide a more convenient working entity than large tables, and they also can provide the necessary security for confidential information in the database.

At the same time, views have some disadvantages. First, they are not stored in the database. Only the view definition is stored in the catalog. The actual view is recomputed each time it is displayed. Therefore views may require more processing time than tables. Moreover, special techniques must be used when UPDATing, INSERTing, or DELETing views based on more than one table. These problems will be discussed as they arise in the sections that follow.

If a view contains a GROUP BY clause or a HAVING clause that is not contained in a subquery, then this is called a *grouped view*.

This chapter will also discuss joining views, using expressions and functions in views, updating views, and using views as part of the data security system.

9.1.1 Creating a View

The syntax for creating a view is:

```
CREATE VIEW        viewname [(view target list)]
AS    SELECT       column1_name,  column2_name, . . .
                   columnN_name
      FROM         tablename
      WHERE        condition
[WITH CHECK OPTION;]
```

The view target list (shown above in brackets after the viewname) does not have to be specified. If it is specified, it must contain the same number of columns in the same order as the target list after the SELECT.

If the view target list is not specified, then no two columns listed after the SELECT can have the same name, and there can be no unnamed columns in the table named after the FROM.

If the view can be updated (see Section 9.1.6 below regarding view updating), then WITH CHECK OPTION can be specified. This option will check that the values inserted as updates fit the WHERE condition. If the view cannot be updated, then the view is considered to be a read-only table.

As an example of the need for creating a view, assume that the original company set up in Chapter 4 has grown so that there are now 12 employees: six salesmen, two clerks, the owner, the secretary, and an accountant. We need to separate the salesmen from the other employees. To do so, we will set up a view called Salesmen, as follows:

```
CREATE VIEW Salesmen
AS    SELECT       name, number, salary, commission
      FROM         employees
      WHERE        job title = ' salesman'
WITH CHECK OPTION;
```

This will give us a view named Salesmen, listing the values shown in the four columns listed after the SELECT statement for only those personnel whose title is salesman. It will look exactly like a base table.

Since the other employees do not receive commissions, using the view will simplify the queries when it is necessary to perform operations relating to the commissions received by the salesmen. At the same time, we can query the view just as we would query any table. If we want to display the contents of the view called Salesmen, we can do it just as we would display all columns of a table:

```
SELECT      *
FROM        Salesmen;
```

The above command will display the view called Salesmen shown below. It was created from the base table Employees:

Salesmen

Employee Name	Employee Number	Salary	Commission
Martin	666 6666	900	975
Jones	555 5555	1200	900
Smith	123 1234	1500	800
Harro	321 4331	1350	950
Fox	222 2424	950	600
Brown	333 4444	850	550

We can use a WHERE clause in querying the view just as we would if it were a base table. For example, if we wanted to display only those salesmen whose salary is higher than a specified figure, we can do it as follows:

```
SELECT      name, salary
FROM        Salesmen
WHERE       salary > 1000;
```

This will produce the following view of the view Salesmen:

Salesmen

Employee Name	Salary
Jones	1200
Smith	1500
Harro	1350

At the same time, since a view itself is not stored, it will be affected by any changes made in the base table from which it is derived. When the table is updated, as for example, if a salesman receives a raise, the next time we query the view, we will find that the view exhibits this updated salary figure for that salesman. If the salesman leaves the company, and his name is deleted from the Employees table, then it will also be deleted from the view Salesmen. If a new salesman is added (inserted) to the Employees table, he will be added to the view Salesmen.

Conversely, if you make changes in a view, some *but not all* such changes will occur back in the base table from which the view was derived. This is an important fact to keep in mind when you are working with views. Changes in views that do not change existing data in the base table are discussed in the appropriate sections below.

9.1.2   Views on More than One Table

You may combine columns from several different tables in any one view. For example, salesmen who live in the same city with a supplier sell the products of that supplier, and it would be convenient to have a view listing these. To do this, join the Name column from the Employees table with the appropriate Name column from the Suppliers table wherever a Salesman is in the same city with the supplier.

This is accomplished as follows:

```
CREATE VIEW        Clients
AS SELECT          employee.name, supplier__name
       FROM        employees, suppliers
       WHERE       title = ' salesman'
       AND         cmployce.city - supplier.city;
```

9.1.3   Joining a View to Another View or to a Table

Views may be joined to each other and/or to a table. The syntax for doing this is shown in Chapter 8. Keep in mind that a view containing a GROUP BY clause cannot be joined to another view or to a table.

9.1.4   Using Expressions and Functions in Views

You can use expressions and functions in a view, but when you do, you must specify names for all the columns in the row. For example, assume we need to convert each employee's monthly salary to an annual salary. We can have the view perform the computation with the following:

```
CREATE VIEW Annual__Salary (employee-name, employee#,
                   address, title, salary)
   AS   SELECT   employee__name, employee#, address, title,
```

```
                salary * 12
    FROM        employees;
```

The computed column "salary * 12" will not appear back in the base table. It will only be available through the view.

Note that there is no ALTER VIEW statement. The ALTER TABLE statement, which adds a column to a table, does not add a column to views that are already defined, although views created after the column is added to the table can show the additional column.

9.1.5 Using Aggregate Functions in Views

You can use all of the aggregate functions, COUNT, COUNT(*), SUM, AVG, MAX, and MIN, in views. (Aggregate functions are defined and discussed in Chapter 7.) For example, to obtain a total amount paid to salesmen, salary must be added to commission. This can be done by using the Salesmen view created in Section 9.1.1 above, as follows:

```
    SELECT      SUM(salary + commission)
    FROM        Salesmen;
```

The result of the above will be a one-column, one-row table showing the total salary plus commission paid to all salesmen.

In the same way, we could use any of the other aggregate functions in the view Salesman, just as though the view were a base table. These calculated columns, however, will not appear back in the base table Employees from which the view Salesmen was drawn.

9.1.6 Updating Rows in Views

If a view is derived from only one table, then instead of updating the base table, you can update the view in the same way you would update the table. For example, the view Salesmen comes directly out of the Employees table; therefore we can update it as follows:

```
    UPDATE      Salesmen
    SET         commission  =  0.25*salary;
```

This UPDATE statement will set the commission of all salesmen at 25 percent of their salaries.

If, however, a view is the result of a join of two or more tables (joins are discussed in Chapter 8), then as with inserting and deleting, updating will require a special process. At present, view updating is a lively topic in the literature, and there are conflicting opinions regarding the best way to handle it. Which way you choose to do it may depend on the capabilities of your user interface to SQL. Therefore, we recommend that you consult the documentation supplied with the implementation you are using, as well as the current literature on this topic. [4,23,27,32,38]. The following restrictions, are offered as cautions rather than as hard and fast rules, since implementors are making breakthroughs in this area.

In general, you may update a view the same way you update a table if:

- It is derived from only one base table.

- It does not contain a GROUP BY clause, or a DISTINCT clause.

- It does not contain any of the group functions AVERAGE, COUNT(*), COUNT, SUM, MAX, or MIN.

- No field of the view is derived from an arithmetic expression or a constant.

9.1.7 Inserting Rows into Views

You may insert rows into views in the same way that you insert rows into tables if the view is derived from only one table.

If the view is the result of a join of two or more tables, then the cautions that were discussed in Section 9.1.6 apply. In general, you can insert rows into views just as you would insert them into tables if:

- The view refers to only one table.

- The view does not contain a GROUP BY clause, a DISTINCT clause, or a group function.

- The view contains no columns defined by the aggregate expressions AVERAGE, COUNT(*), COUNT, MAX, MIN, or SUM.

9.1.8 Deleting Rows from Views

The cautions that applied to updating and inserting data in views also apply to deleting data from views, except that you can DELETE from a view derived from an arithmetic expression or a constant.

In general you may delete rows from views the same way that you delete rows from tables if:

- The view is derived from only one table.

- The view does not contain a GROUP BY clause, a DISTINCT clause, or an aggregate function (such as AVERAGE or COUNT).

9.1.9 Using Views to Restrict Table Access

Views can be used to divide up the database into column or row segments of tables. Then, by using the DCL GRANT and REVOKE statements, you can hide confidential information from all but authorized users. For example, if a new user were to be allowed to work with employees' names, titles, and employee numbers, but not with their salaries, the following view could be created:

```
CREATE VIEW        Employees__Limited
AS
          SELECT   employee__name, employee#, title
          FROM     employees;
```

The new user could then be granted access to this view rather than to the complete Employees table, where all personnel data are stored, with the following command:

```
GRANT    SELECT, UPDATE(Title) ON EMPLOYEES__LIMITED
TO       new__user, new__userid;
```

If the new user's privileges are to be more extensive, the following command can be used:

```
GRANT    ALL PRIVILEGES ON EMPLOYEES__LIMITED
TO       new__user, new__userid;
```

In this way, confidential information can be hidden in the table, while nonconfidential information can be available in the same table to users who need to work with it.

9.2 Using SQL to Optimize Performance

Indices have two main purposes:

- To improve performance by reducing disk I/O. Indices in a database perform a function similar to that of the Indices in a book: they speed up the retrieval of information. This is especially true for information in joined tables.

- To insure uniqueness. You can create a unique index on a column. Then, if an attempt is made to insert a row that will duplicate a value already in that column, the insertion will be rejected. Therefore, a UNIQUE INDEX acts as a check on the uniqueness of the column.

9.2.1 Indices and Keys

While the use of SQL requires an index, it does not require a key. Keys, however, are a part of relational databases, but currently they are rarely implemented except through indices. A *candidate key* is a designated column (or group of columns) that can be used to uniquely define a row in a given table. One of the candidate keys can be designated as the *primary key*. A *foreign key* is a designated column in a given table that can be used to uniquely define a row in some other table, i.e., a candidate key in some other table.

If your implementation makes use of keys, then creating an index on each key will definitely improve query performance. Update performance will not necessarily be improved and may even be reduced by indices, because the index has to be recomputed after each update. There is, however, another reason for maintaining a unique index on all candidate keys: A properly designed database scheme usually has the property that integrity of the database requires that all candidate keys always determine a unique row. In most current implementations, the only way to guarantee this is to define a unique index on every candidate key. For more information on maintaining integrity constraints by means of candidate keys, refer to Maier's treatment of complete database schemes *[46]*.

9.2.2 UNIQUE Indices

If you own a table (i.e., if you created the table) or if you have been granted access to a table, you can create an index on it. The syntax for creating a UNIQUE index is:

```
CREATE UNIQUE INDEX index_name
ON table_name
    column_name(s);
```

where the column names are those columns you want indexed.

You can index as many columns of a table as you wish, but how many columns you index will depend on the purpose of the table: if the table is to be updated frequently, then more indices mean more overhead. If, on the other hand, it is a read-only table, or is seldom updated, then it would be advisable to have more indices.

9.2.3 Indices on More than One Column

If you need to ensure uniqueness across several columns (for example, in tables in which it takes more than one column to uniquely identify a row), then you can concatenate the indices on those columns. Concatenated indices speed retrieval if you frequently include a WHERE clause in your queries specifying that group of columns. The syntax is:

```
CREATE UNIQUE INDEX index__name ON table__name
(column1__name, column2__name, . . . , columnN__name);
```

where the column names are those you want concatenated. This index will speed retrieval on queries combining those same columns (in that same order) in the WHERE clause, such as

```
WHERE     column1__name     = 'constant'
AND       column2__name     = 'constant'
AND       columnN__name     = 'constant';
```

The two main ways of accessing data are by using a full table scan and by using an index. Using the index will usually result in higher performance because most SQL statements are set up to retrieve only a few specified rows of a table. If, however, the retrieval consists of a large portion of the table, using the index will only increase the overhead.

9.3 Optimizing Queries

While the implementation will determine the access paths, you can influence its choice by the construction of your SQL query. Since there are usually several different ways to write a SQL query, the following points should be used as guidelines:

- An index will not be used if there is no WHERE clause in the statement.

- If the WHERE clause contains either IS NULL or IS NOT NULL, an index will not be used.

- Indices are more likely to be used on columns defined as NOT NULL.

- A column defined as UNIQUE and NOT NULL fullfils the requirements for a key (whether or not your implementation makes use of keys) and therefore can enhance performance.

In general, system optimizers will process non-nested queries (i.e., queries not containing subqueries) more efficiently than they will nested queries. The complexities of this subject are detailed in work presented by Kim [41].

Exercises

Assume that you have an Employees table, a Customer table, and a Suppliers table in the following exercises.

9.1 Create a view of the employees table showing Employee Name, Employee Number, and Title for all employees who are not salesmen.

9.2 Create a view showing the average commission received by each salesman.

9.3 Create a view showing the total commission received by each salesman.

9.4 Can the view created in Exercise 9.2 above be updated?

9.5 Create a view of salesmen and the companies they service.

9.6 Can you insert a new row into the view you set up in Exercise 9.1?

9.7 Can you delete a row from the view created in Exercise 9.5 above?

9.8 Create a view showing the annual salary of all employees from the base table showing monthly salaries.

9.9 Can you update the view created in Exercise 9.8 above?

9.10 Can you delete a row from the view created in Exercise 9.8 above?

Answers to Exercises

```
9.1 CREATE VIEW non__sales
        AS    SELECT     *
              FROM       employees
              WHERE      NOT title = ' salesman';
```

(The above WHERE clause could be entered as

> WHERE   title < > ' salesman';)

9.2 CREATE VIEW salesmen
```
      AS    SELECT     AVG(commission*12)
            FROM       employees
            WHERE      title = ' salesman';
```

9.3 CREATE VIEW salesmen
```
      AS    SELECT     SUM(commission)
            FROM       employees
            WHERE      title = ' salesman';
```

9.4 No, because it contains a column based on an aggregate function.

9.5 CREATE VIEW clients
```
      AS    SELECT     salesman__name, customer__name
            FROM       employees, customers
            WHERE      employee.title = ' salesmen'
            AND        salesman.district = customer.district;
```

9.6 Yes.

9.7 No, because it is derived from more than one table.

9.8 CREATE VIEW annual__salary
```
      AS SELECT employee__name,(salary*12)
            FROM         employees;
```

9.9 No, because it contains a column based on an arithmetic expression.

9.10 Yes.

10

The Relational Algebra and SQL

WHILE SQL HAS BEEN SAID TO RESEMBLE THE TUPLE RELATIONAL CALculus, SQL also owes much to the relational algebra. In this chapter we develop the relevant parts of relational algebra and give corresponding SQL queries to show the relationship between SQL and the relational algebra.

Given a finite set of attributes $U = \{A_1, A_2, \ldots, A_u\}$ with domains $dom(A_i)$, a relation scheme is a subset of U. A relational database scheme D over U is a collection of relation schemes, $\{R_1, R_2, \ldots, R_d\}$, such that the union of the R_i is U. Given a relation scheme R, a tuple, t, over R is a single-valued mapping from the members of R to the domains of the members of R such that $t(A_i)$ is a member of $dom(A_i)$ for A_i a member of R. A relation over a relation scheme R is a finite set of tuples over R.

Relations over a relation scheme R are frequently displayed as rectangular tables in which the column headings are the members of R and the rows are tuples such that, if t is a tuple, then $t(A_i)$ is entered in the row corresponding to t and the column corresponding to A_i.

10.1 Relational Definitions

If $S_1, S_2, \ldots, S_k$ are sets, then a tuple on $S_1, S_2, \ldots, S_k$ is an expression $(s_1, s_2, \ldots, s_k)$ where s_i is a member of S_i for $i = 1, 2, .$

. .,k. The cartesian product $S_1 \times S_2 \times \ldots \times S_k$ is the set of all such tuples. A tuple may also be thought of as a function f from the set labels $S_1, S_2, \ldots, S_k$ into the sets $S_1, S_2, \ldots, S_k$ such that the value of f at S_i is a member of S_i. Thus, if t is a tuple and A is an attribute, we can write $t[A]$ to denote the value of t at A. This notation is particularly useful in the case of a relation scheme R over the attributes $A_1, A_2, \ldots, A_k$. Then the members of a relation r over the scheme R are tuples over the A_is.

The following is an example:

If R = {A,B,C} where Dom(A) = Dom(B) = Dom(C) = the set of integers, and r is the relation

A	B	C
1	1	1
2	3	1

then, we may think of r as consisting of the tuples t and u where $t[A] = 1$, $t[B] = 1$, $t[C] = 1$, $u[A] = 2$, $u[B] = 3$, and $u[C] = 1$.

10.2   Boolean Operators

The Boolean operators in the relational algebra are union ($\cup$), intersection $\cap$) and difference ($-$). These operators can only be applied between two relations having the same relation schemes. The union of two relations is the set of all tuples that are in either one. The intersection is the set of all tuples that are in both; and the difference is the set of all tuples that are in one but not the other.

The following is an example:

Let r_1 and r_2 be the two following relations:

	r_1				r_2	
A	B	C		A	B	C
1	1	1		3	3	3
2	2	2		1	4	9
3	3	3		3	3	2

Then the union, $r_1 \cup r_2$, is:

```
A   B   C
1   1   1
2   2   2
3   3   3
1   4   9
3   3   2
```

The intersection, $r_1 \cap r_2$, is:

```
A   B   C
3   3   3
```

The difference, $r_1 - r_2$, is:

```
A   B   C
1   1   1
2   2   2
```

SQL has union but not intersection and difference. For example, to get the union we could write

```
SELECT *
FROM R₁
UNION
SELECT *
FROM r₂;
```

Getting the intersection and difference can be achieved in SQL by using the logical connectives AND, OR, and NOT and EXISTS, but the process is much more complicated than getting the union. See Chapter 8 and the exercises at the end of this chapter.

10.3   The Projection Operator

Given a relation r on relation scheme R, the projection, s, of r on some subset S of R is the restriction of the tuples in R to the members of S. We denote the projection on S by π_S. The following is an example:

Let r be the relation

```
A   B   C
1   1   1
1   2   3
3   2   1
```

Then we have

$\pi_{\{A,B\}}r$		$\pi_{\{A,C\}}r$		$\pi_{\{B\}}r$
A	B	A	C	B
1	1	1	1	1
1	2	1	3	2
3	2	3	1	

Repeated rows are removed. That is why $\pi_{\{B\}}$ has only two rows. In SQL, projection is achieved by means of the target list—in other words, by selecting only those columns of the subscheme that we want.

10.4   The Select Operator

The select operator, $\varrho_{A=a}$, operates on a relation r to give the subrelation of those tuples t such that $t[A] = a$, for some constant value a. The following is an example:

Let r be the relation

A	B	C
1	1	2
1	2	1
2	3	2

Then $\varrho_{B=1}$ is

A	B	C
1	1	2

The corresponding SQL query expression is.

```
SELECT *
FROM r
WHERE B = 1;
```

10.5   The Join Operator

Given two relations r_1 and r_2 on relation schemes R_1 and R_2, we define the join of r_1 and r_2 to be a relation r on the union of R_1 and R_2. Namely, it is those tuples whose projection on R_1 match some tuple of r_1, and whose projection on R_2 match some tuple of r_2. The join of r_1 and r_2 is denoted $r_1 \bowtie r_2$. The following is an example:

If r_1 and r_2 are the relations

A	B	C	D
1	1	1	1
2	2	1	3
1	2	5	3
1	2	3	4

B	D	E
1	1	1
2	3	6
1	1	5
4	3	2

Then $r_1 \bowtie r_2$ is

A	B	C	D	E
1	1	1	1	1
1	1	1	1	5
2	2	1	3	6
1	2	5	3	6

Notice that some rows in the original relations appear more than once in the join, while others may not appear at all.

The above join may be written in SQL as follows.

```
SELECT A,B,C,D,E
FROM r₁,r₂
WHERE r₁.B = r₂.B
AND r₁.D = r₂.D
```

It is apparent from the above SQL expression that the join is a special case of the equijoin. (See Chapter 8 for a definition of the equijoin.) The relational algebra also has join operators involving comparators other than equals. These are called θ joins, and are defined exactly in the same way as the equijoin except that $=$ is replaced with $<$, $>$, $\leq$, $<$, or $>$.

10.6 The Division of Relations (Lossy Joins)

If we think of the join as a generalized multiplication for relations, then we would like to have an operator analogous to division. Let r be a relation over the scheme R and s be a relation over the scheme S where S is a subset of R. For each scheme S' such that S union

S' equals R, we would like to find a relation s' such that s⋈s' equals r. In general that is impossible. The following is an example:

Let r and s be the relations.

r				s	
A	B	C		A	B
1	2	3		1	4

There is no relation on any subset of {A,B,C} that will join with s to produce r. That is because the tuple in s is not the projection on {A,B} of any tuple in s.

In view of the above example, let us confine ourselves to division when s is the result of a projection operating on r. The following is an example:

Let r be the relation shown below, and let s and s' be $\pi_{\{A,B\}}r$ and $\pi_{\{A,C\}}r$, respectively.

r				s			s'	
A	B	C		A	B		A	C
1	2	3		1	2		1	3
1	3	4		1	3		1	4

Then s⋈s' is

s⋈s'		
A	B	C
1	2	3
1	2	4
1	3	3
1	3	4

Clearly, s⋈s' contains the rows in r plus two additional rows, and is thus not equal to r. This is an example of a *lossy join*. The term *lossy join* is misleading since a lossy join always contains more rows than the original relation. If you repeat the operation by projecting on {A,B} and {A,C}, and then join again, you get the relation s⋈s' back again.

Thus, there is no easy way to define an operator analogous to division. In the relational database literature (See, for example, Maier[46]), the division operator is defined as follows:

Let r be a relation on the scheme R, and s be a relation on the scheme S where S is a subset of R. Let $s' = r \div s$ be the largest relation on the scheme R − S such that $s \div s'$ is a subrelation of r. Since S and R − S are disjoint, $s \div s'$ is the cartesian product of s and s'. The following is an example:

Let r and s be as in the previous example. The expression r ÷ s is clearly the relation on {C} that has no rows, the *empty relation*.

Division is frequently used in database queries to find those objects that have certain properties. For example, if you have the relation scheme R = {prisoner_name,charge}, and you want to find those prisoners charged with driving in a less-than-sober condition, the following query will get them:

```
SELECT prisoner_name
FROM prisoners
WHERE charge = 'DUI';
```

In effect, the above query divides any relation over R by the relation:

```
charge
'DUI'.
```

10.7   The Literature on Relational Algebra

Both Maier[46] and Yang[55] have complete treatments of the relational algebra. Codd[17] defined the relational algebra giving the operators named here; he also defined relational completeness in terms of the relational algebra. Date[26] outlines a proof that SQL is relationally complete, i.e., that every operation in the relational algebra can be performed in SQL.

Exercises

10.1. Let the relations r_1 and r_2 be

r_1			r_2	
A	B		A	B
1	1		3	5
3	5		1	2
5	6		2	9

    a. Find the union, intersection, and difference.
    b. Write a SQL query expression for the union.
    c. Write a SQL query expression for the intersection.
    d. Write a SQL query expression for the difference.

10.2. Given a relation r over the relation scheme {prisoner_
      name,charge}, let s be the relation

    charge
    ' DUI'
    ' ARSON'

    Find a SQL expression for $r \div s$

10.3. Given the relations r, s, and t as follows:

r		s		t	
A	B	B	C	C	A
1	2	3	4	5	6
2	3	5	6	4	2
1	5	3	1	1	2
7	8	2	4	4	1

    Compute $(r \bowtie s) \bowtie t$ and show that it is the same as $r \bowtie (s \bowtie t)$.

10.4 Compute the join of r and s where r and s are

r		s	
A	B	C	D
1	2	1	2
2	4	2	3

Answers to Exercises

10.1a. The union intersection and difference, in that order, are

A	B	A	B	A	B
1	1	3	5	1	1
3	5			5	6
5	6				
1	2				
2	9				

b. SELECT *
   FROM r_1
   UNION
   SELECT *
   FROM r_2;

c. SELECT *
   FROM r_1
   WHERE EXISTS
   (SELECT *
   FROM r_2
   WHERE $r_1.A = r_2.A$
   AND $r_1.B = r_2.B$);

d. SELECT *
   FROM r_1
   WHERE NOT EXISTS
   (SELECT *
   FROM r_2
   WHERE $r_1.A = r_2.A$
   AND $r_1.B = r_2.B$);

10.2 SELECT prisoner_name
     FROM R
     WHERE charge = ' DUI'
     AND charge = ' ARSON';

is wrong, since there cannot be two charges in a single row. The following is one possible correct query using a subquery.

SELECT prisoner_name
FROM R
WHERE charge = ' DUI'
AND prisoner_name IN
(SELECT prisoner_name
FROM R
WHERE charge = ' ARSON');

10.3

A	B	C
1	2	4
2	3	4
2	3	1

10.4

A	B	C	D
1	2	1	2
1	2	2	3
2	4	1	2
2	4	2	3

This is the Cartesian product.

11

Logic and SQL

LET US RECONSIDER QUERIES. WHAT IS A QUERY? SUPPOSE YOU HAVE A
database consisting of shipments of auto parts to various locations
throughout the US and you want to know what parts you shipped
to the dealer in Cleveland on Thursday. You might like to ask the
computer: "Give me a list of parts shipped to the dealer in Cleveland on Thursday." If, however, you type that in you'll get nothing.
The software available today is incapable of interpreting a simple
request unless it is formulated in some fixed, limited, "formal" language.

Since queries such as the one in the preceding paragraph
contemplate a set of things (perhaps two left fenders and a brake
shoe) as the answer, it is desirable for the formal language to be
able to determine sets as answers.

First-order logic was developed by mathematicians in the first
part of this century and the latter part of the previous century for
the purpose of studying the foundations and consistency of mathematics.
This was necessary at the time because mathematicians had been
plagued by paradoxes. First-order logic aimed at developing a consistent
set theory and thus contained a language for describing sets. For
a treatment of first-order logic see Church[13] or Mendelson[49].

The first-order logic for describing sets was ideal as a first step
toward a query language for querying about sets. A part of it was
first adopted by Codd[17] in 1971 for queries on relational databases.

Codd called his development *the relational calculus*, and called his queries *alpha expressions*. He then showed that alpha expressions could be converted to operations in the relational algebra. In the recent literature (See, for example, Maier[46] and Yang[55], the relational calculus comes in two flavors: tuple relational calculus and domain relational calculus. In tuple relational calculus, the variables refer to tuples, or rows in relations. In domain relational calculus the variables refer to attributes instead of rows. Codd's relational calculus is like the tuple relational calculus.

This chapter contains a brief overview of the entire development, starting with the propositional calculus and ending with a slightly modified version of Codd's relational calculus. To show how SQL resembles the tuple relational calculus, examples and exercises are given involving the creation of alpha expressions to represent queries and the conversion of these alpha expressions to SQL.

11.1 Relational Definitions

Given a finite set of attributes $U = \{A_1, A_2, \ldots, A_u\}$ with domains $dom(A_i)$, a relation scheme is a subset of U. A relational database scheme D over U is a collection of relation schemes, $\{R_1, R_2, \ldots, R_d\}$, such that the union of the R_i is U. Given a relation scheme R, a tuple, t, over R is a single-valued mapping from the members of R to the domains of the members of R such that $t(A_i)$ is a member of $dom(A_i)$ for A_i a member of R. A relation over a relation scheme R is a finite set of tuples over R.

Relations over a relation scheme R are frequently displayed as rectangular tables in which the column headings are the members of R and the rows are tuples such that, if t is a tuple, then $t(A_i)$ is entered in the row corresponding to t and the column corresponding to A_i. The following is an example:

If $R = \{A,B,C\}$ where $Dom(A) = Dom(B) = Dom(C) =$ the set of integers, and r is the relation

A	B	C
1	1	1
2	3	1

then, we may think of r as consisting of the tuples t and u where $t[A] = 1$, $t[B] = 1$, $t[C] = 1$, $u[A] = 2$, $u[B] = 3$, and $u[C] = 1$.

11.2   Formal Theory

In mathematical logic, an entity known as a *formal theory* is defined in the following way.

1. An infinite set of symbols S is given. A finite sequence of these symbols is called an *expression*.

2. Some expressions are called *well-formed formulas* (wfs). We will call a single well-formed formula a "wff."

3. Some of the wfs are designated as *axioms*.

4. A finite set of *rules of inference* is given whereby some wfs can be derived from others. For example, "from A implies B and A we can derive B" is a rule of inference known as *modus ponens*.

5. A *proof* is a sequence of wfs such that each is either an axiom or can be derived from those preceding it by one of the rules of inference.

6. A *theorem* is the last member of a proof.

A query language only uses numbers 1 and 2 above. The rest are included here for completeness. In addition to 1 and 2, a query language requires a well-defined interpretation.

11.3   Interpretations

Everyone is familiar with the idea of an *interpretation*. Frequently, after listening to someone speak we ask someone else for their interpretation of what was said. We might ask "How do you interpret that?" If someone speaks of a cat, we might think of a particular cat. That is another way of interpreting what they said. Another kind of interpretation is deciding whether or not a statement is true or false (or plausible). A formal theory is given meaning by means of an interpretation without which it is simply a meaningless collection of sequences of symbols.

In mathematics, an interpretation is simply a function that maps the symbols in a formal theory to something else that usually has more meaning. As we will see, the idea of an interpretation plays an important role in both first-order logic and the relational calculus. Namely, the answer to a query is those rows of a relation for which the conditions of the query are interpreted to be true or satisfied.

If we have a query language in which a particular query cannot be interpreted to be satisfied or not satified, then that query cannot be executed in the given query language.

11.4   The Propositional Calculus

The set of symbols used in propositional calculus is as follows:

- An infinite set of statement letters A_i for i = 1 to infinity.
- The three primitive connectives AND, OR, and NOT.
- Right and left parentheses.

The rules for forming well-formed formulas (wfs) are:

- All statement letters are wfs.
- If X and Y are wfs, then so are (NOT X), (X AND Y), and (X OR Y).

These rules may be repeated any number of times. For example, if A and B are statement letters, then A is a wff and B is a wff. Applying rule 2 we see that (NOT A) is a wff. Applying rule 2 again ((NOT A) AND B) is seen to be a wff, and so on. This type of definition is said to be a *recursive* definition. In this chapter all definitions with rules will be understood to be recursive; that is, the rules may be repeated an arbitrary number of times.

Frequently in the logic literature, the rule, "Nothing else is a . . ." is added to the list of rules for recursive definitions. To avoid repeating this rule everywhere a recursive definition occurs, it should be understood that "Nothing else is a . . ." wherever we have a recursive definition.

The main interpretation for the propositional calculus is a set of mappings, called *truth functions*, from wfs to the set TF = {TRUE,FALSE}. Given a wff W, first we define functions on the statement letters to the set TF. Then by repeated use of the following tables, we find a mapping of W to TF.

A	NOT A
TRUE	FALSE
FALSE	TRUE

A	B	A AND B
TRUE	TRUE	TRUE
TRUE	FALSE	FALSE
FALSE	TRUE	FALSE
FALSE	FALSE	FALSE

A	B	A OR B
TRUE	TRUE	TRUE
TRUE	FALSE	TRUE
FALSE	TRUE	TRUE
FALSE	FALSE	FALSE

Notice that the OR is nonexclusive.

IMPLIES can be added to AND, OR, and NOT, and is defined as follows: (A IMPLIES B) equals ((NOT A) OR B). This definition, while similar to, is not exactly the same as the way that implication is usually defined in everyday language, as will be demonstrated. From the definition given here we obtain (by substitution) the truth table

A	B	A IMPLIES B
TRUE	TRUE	TRUE
TRUE	FALSE	FALSE
FALSE	TRUE	TRUE
FALSE	FALSE	TRUE

so that this IMPLIES is true when the premise is false or the conclusion is true, even if the premise has no relationship whatsoever to the conclusion. In everyday language, the formation of the sentence A IMPLIES B is not even contemplated when A has no relationship to B. For example, one would not form the sentence "My dog is a unicorn implies oranges are apples." However, since the premise is false, this sentence is true in the propositional calculus. Furthermore, since the propositional calculus (with statement letters replaced by predicates) is a part of first-order logic which, in turn, forms a foundation for modern mathematics, modern mathematics involves the type of implication defined here. This fact may seem confusing, especially in the case of statements such as "Every element of the empty set has the value two," which is true since the empty set has no elements. In other words "x is a member of the empty set implies x = 2" is true in mathematics because the statement "x is a member of the empty set" is false, and a false premise implies any conclusion. The motivation for this meaning for implies is to fit implies into a two-valued logic. Essentially it does no harm because mathematicians are not concerned about implications where the premise is false. Of course, mathematics is not confined to two-valued logic, but that is another story, one we shall not go into here.

The following is an example:

Consider the wff W:

(((A IMPLIES B) AND (B IMPLIES C)) IMPLIES (A IMPLIES C)).

If we assign TRUE to A, FALSE to B and FALSE to C, then (A IMPLIES B) has the value FALSE and (B IMPLIES C) has the value TRUE. Thus, ((A IMPLIES B) AND (B IMPLIES C)) has the value FALSE, and the entire wff has the value TRUE.

Consequently, for this assignment of values to the statement letters, W has the value TRUE. As it turns out, W has the value TRUE for any assignment of values to the variables. In the propositional calculus a wff with this property is called a *tautology*. The tautologies of propositional calculus are exactly the theorems of propositional calculus. Thus, this interpretation of the propositional calculus along with the use of truth tables turns out to be an effective means for determining whether or not a given wff is a theorem. We have left out the axioms and rules of inference for propositional calculus because they are not needed here. For a more extensive treatment of the propositional calculus see Mendelson[49] or Church[13].

11.5 Predicates and Quantifiers

In symbolic logic it is necessary to be able to assert that something has a given property or that two or more things have a certain relationship. Properties and relationships are called *predicates*. "Bill is John's brother" and "That is a donkey" are examples of predicates. We can write B(b,j) to stand for "Bill is John's brother," where b stands for Bill, j stands for John, and B(x,y) is the predicate "x is the brother of y." Here B(,), b, and j are constants, while x and y are variables and can have various constants substituted for them. We could also write D(x) to stand for "x is a donkey," where D( ) is a constant predicate and x is a variable. B is a two-place or binary predicate, and D is a single-place or monadic predicate.

126

In order to accommodate these new parts of language, we need to extend our previous definitions for wfs. In first-order logic, the letters from the beginning of the alphabet, $a,b,c,..$ are used for constants, and letters from the end of the alphabet, x,y,z, for variables. There is an infinite list of *function letters* f_i. Each f_i will have an integer $n_i > = 1$ associated with it; and f will thus be said to be *an n-place function* where $n = n_i$. Further, there is an infinite number of predicate letters P_i, and each P_i will also have an integer $m_i > = 1$ associated with it where m_i is the number of arguments associated with it.

Terms are defined as follows:

- Variables and constants are terms.
- If f_i is an n-place function and $t_1,t_2,...,t_n$ are terms then

$$f(t_1,t_2,...,t_n)$$

is a term.

Atomic formulas are defined to be n-place predicates with n terms filled in. For example, if P is an n-place predicate, then $P(t_1,t_2,...,t_n)$ is an atomic formula.

Examples of functions are plus and times. For example if $f(x,y)$ stands for $x + y$, then $f(3,4) = 7$.

$P(x)$ can stand for an n-place predicate having x as a variable. Quantifiers in this context are *for all* and *there exists*. We will write *for all* as (x) where x is a variable. Then $(x)P(x)$ means "for all x the predicate P holds." We will write $E(x)$ to stand for "There exists an x such that . . ." so that $E(x)P(x)$ stands for "There exists an x such that P holds for x," or just "There exists an x such that P of x."

The well-formed formulas (wfs) are built up as follows:

- Every atomic formula is a wff.
- If X is a wff then (NOT X) is a wff.
- If X and Y are wfs then (X AND Y) is a wff.
- If X and Y are wfs then (X OR Y) is a wff.
- If X is a wff then ((x)X) is a wff.
- If X is a wff then (E(x)X) is a wff.

If, in the propositional calculus, we replace statement letters by predicates with terms filled in, we obtain a subset of the predicate calculus. This can be seen by noticing that the first four rules above for wfs are the same as for the propositional calculus.

In ((x)X), where X is a wff, X is called the scope of (x) because (x) and X are within the same outer parentheses. In the case of (((x)X) AND Y) Y is "not within the scope of (x)." If X does not contain the variable x then ((x)X) is to be replaced by X.

E(x) could be dispensed with because (E(x)X) is taken to be the same as (NOT ((x)(NOT X))); however, we shall keep E(x) since it makes some expressions briefer.

11.6 Free and Bound Variables

It is important to distinguish between free and bound variables because the two types are interpreted differently. Therefore, we have the following technical definition.

An occurrence of a variable x in a wff X is said to be bound in X if (x) (or E(x)) occurs in X and the occurrence of x is within the scope of (x) (or E(x)). Also an occurrence of (x) or E(x) is said to be *bound*. If an occurrence of a variable x in X is not within the scope of a quantifier (x) or E(x), then that occurrence of x is said to be "free" in X. The following is an example:

In $A(x_1,x_2)$ OR $(x_1)B(x_1)$ the occurrence of x_1 in A is free and the occurrence of x_1 in B is bound. The occurrence of x_1 in (x_1) is also bound.

We modify the last two rules above for wfs by allowing ((x)X) and (E(x)X) only when x has a free occurrence in X.

11.7 Interpretations for the Predicate Calculus

The development in this section is based on papers in Tarski[52]. See also Mendelson[49] and Church[13].

In the first-order logic an interpretation consists of:

- A non-empty set S called the *domain* of the interpretation.

- An assignment to each n-place predicate of an n-place relation on S. A relation on S is a set of n-tuples of S. For example, if S is the set of integers, then the relation "greater than" is the set of all ordered pairs (i,j) such that i is greater than j.

- An assignment to each n-place function of an n-place function on S into S.

- An assignment to each constant letter of an element of S.

Given a wff W having n variables $x_1, x_2, ..., x_n$ and a sequence SEQ $b_1, b_2, ..., b_n$ of n members of S (possibly with repeats), check whether or not "SEQ satisfies W" as follows:

1. Wherever x_i occurs in W, substitute b_i for it.

2. Wherever a constant occurrs in W, substitute the corresponding member of S given by the fourth rule above.

3. For each function in W, perform the corresponding function on S, given by the third rule above, and replace the function by the resulting element of S.

4. For each predicate P in W, check to see that the tuple of members of S in P is a tuple in the relation given by the second rule above. If so, replace P by SATISFIED; otherwise replace P by NOT SATISFIED.

5. Replace (NOT (SATISFIED)) by (NOT SATISFIED) and replace (NOT (NOT SATISFIED)) by (SATISFIED).

6. Replace:
   ((SATISFIED) AND (SATISFIED)) by (SATISFIED),
   ((SATISFIED) AND (NOT SATISFIED)) by (NOT SATISFIED),
   ((NOT SATISFIED) AND (SATISFIED)) by (NOT SATISFIED),
   and
   ((NOT SATISFIED) AND (NOT SATISFIED)) by (NOT SATISFIED).

7. Replace:
   ((SATISFIED) OR (SATISFIED)) by (SATISFIED),
   ((SATISFIED) OR (NOT SATISFIED)) by (SATISFIED),
   ((NOT SATISFIED) OR (SATISFIED)) by (SATISFIED), and
   ((NOT SATISFIED) OR (NOT SATISFIED)) by (NOT SATISFIED).

8. Replace (x_i)X by SATISFIED if every sequence of n elements from S, that differs from SEQ in at most the ith element results in X being replaced by SATISFIED. Otherwise, replace (x_i)X by NOT SATISFIED.

9. Replace $E(x_i)$X by SATISFIED if there exists a sequence of n elements from S, that differs from SEQ in at most the ith element such that it results in X being replaced by SATISFIED. Otherwise, replace $E(x_i)$X by NOT SATISFIED.

By repeated use of 1 through 9, the wff W will eventually be replaced either by SATISFIED or NOT SATISFIED. If W is replaced by SATISFIED, we say "SEQ satisfies W."

If W is a wff with n variables and I is an interpretation of W with domain S, then W is said to be "true with respect to I" if W is satisfied by every n element sequence from S. W is said to be "false with respect to I" if W is not satisfied by any n element sequence from S.

If G is a set of wfs and I is an interpretation for all the wfs in G, such that each wff in G is true with respect to I, then, I is said to be a "model for G." The theory of models plays an important role in modern mathematics. For examples related to relations see Cohn[22].

In the last 25 years a new approach to the foundations of mathematics, logic, interpretations, and models, has developed in a subject area of mathematics called *category theory*. This development promises to have great significance for query languages and computer science. Category theory is, however, beyond the scope of this book. For more information consult Makkai and Reyes[47] and Barr and Wells[5].

Recently, more and more logical systems are being used in computer science. This development is called logic programming. The 1984 article by Goguen and Burstall[33] is a good starting point for anyone who would like to know more about logic programming.

11.8 Tuple Relational Calculus

In his 1971 article [17] Codd, having in mind a query language for relational databases using concepts of first-order logic, developed what he called the *relational calculus*. Given a database scheme D, he limited his predicates, terms, and wfs based on D. Then he defined an interpretation of the resulting calculus in such a way that each wff corresponded to a query whose result is those tuples that satisfy the wff. We shall do what Codd did but in a slightly different manner to maintain a greater similarity to the development of first-order logic.

In the following we assume a universe of attributes $U = \{A_1, A_2, \ldots, A_k\}$, and a database scheme $D = \{R_1, R_2, \ldots, R_j\}$, where each R_i is a relation scheme over some subset of the attributes in U. Furthermore, we assume a finite relation r_i over each relation scheme R_i.

Given D, we start with an interpretation whose set S of elements is the union of the relations over the relation schemes in D. There will be an infinite set of variables x_i, $i >= 1$ and an infinite set of constants $a_i, i >= 1$. For each attribute A_i in U let f_i be a function letter. There will be l unary predicates $P_1, P_2, \ldots, P_l$. The meaning of $P_i(x)$ is "x is a tuple in r_i". In other words, in our interpretation $P_i(x)$ is SATISFIED if and only if x is a tuple in r_i. There will be five binary predicates $P_=$, $P_>$, $P_<$, $P_{<=}$, and $P_{>=}$.

Terms will be either variables or $f(x)$ where x is a variable and f is a function. If P is a unary predicate and x is a variable, then $P(x)$ is an atomic formula. If P is one of the binary predicates, f_i and f_j are function letters, x and y are variables, and the domains of A_i and A_j are comparable, then $P(f_i(x), f_j(y))$ is an atomic formula. Similarly, $P(f_i(x), a)$ is an atomic formula where a is constrained to be interpreted into values that are comparable to those in the domain of A_i.

The meaning of $P_C(f_i(x), f_j(y))$ is "$f_i(x) \, C \, f_j(y)$" where C is one of the comparators $=$, $>$, $<$, $<=$, $>=$. In other words, if, in our interpretation, x is mapped into a tuple u and y is mapped into a tuple v such that the value of u at attribute i is in the relationship C to the value of v at j, then $P_C(f_i(x), f_j(y))$ is SATISFIED, and otherwise $P_C(f_i(x), f_j(y))$ is NOT SATISFIED. Similarly the meaning of $P_C(f_i(x), a)$ is "$f_i(x) \, C \, a$" where the obvious rule holds for SATISFIED and NOT SATISFIED.

Given these atomic formulas, we define simple wfs as follows:

- Every simple wff must be of the form

  U_1 AND U_2 AND . . . AND U_n AND V

  where each U_i is $P(x)$ for some unary predicate P and every free variable in V appears in one of the U_i.

  Thus, in our interpretation, if x is a free variable then x must appear in P_i for some i, and thus x must be mapped into a member of S that is also a member of r_i. In other words, the U_i merely tell us what tables the tuple variables belong to.

  Furthermore, if x is a variable that appears in P_i then $f_j(x)$ is allowed only if A_j is a member of R_i (We say j is "acceptable for x").

  Then, if x is mapped into the tuple t in r_i, $f_j(t) = t(A_j)$.

If *a* is a constant variable, then *a* will be mapped into a member of the domain of some attribute in U. If two terms occur in a binary predicate, then they must be comparable. For example, strings are not to be compared with numbers. Similarly, if a term and *a* constant letter a occur in a binary predicate, they must be comparable.

- If *x* is a bound variable appearing in V within the scope of a quantifier Q(x), then there must be a unary predicate P such that P(x) appears within the scope of Q, but NOT P(x) does not appear within the scope of Q, and no other unary predicate P′ with *x* in it occurs within the scope of Q. This rule is clearly necessary to determine the interpretation of *x*, namely those tuples that *x* can be mapped into or to put it another way, the table in the database to which the variable x refers.

11.9   Simple Alpha Expressions

Following Codd, we define a *simple alpha expression* as an expression of the form $(t_1, t_2, \ldots, t_k) : w$

where

- *w* is a simple wff.

- $t_1, t_2, \ldots, t_k$ are distinct terms each being a free variable in *w* or being $f_i(x)$ where *x* is a free variable in *w*, and *i* is acceptable for *x*. Codd calls this list of terms the *target list*.

- The set of variables occurring in $t_1, t_2, \ldots, t_k$ corresponds exactly to the set of free variables in *w*. The list $(t_1, t_2, \ldots, t_k)$ is called the target list, and *w* is called the *qualification expression*.

11.10   Alpha Expressions

Following Codd, we generalize the notion of simple alpha expressions to alpha expressions as follows

- Every simple alpha expression is an alpha expression.

- If $t:w_1$ and $t:w_2$ are alpha expressions then

    t: $(w_1 \text{ OR } w_2)$,

t: (w_1 AND (NOT w_2)), and
t: (w_1 AND w_2)

are alpha expressions.

The following is an example:

I. Let D be a database scheme over the set of attributes U = {flight_number,type_of_plane,gate_number}, with relation schemes

Type = {flight_number,type_of_plane}, and Gate = {flight_number, gate_number}.

Let the relations for Type and Gate be as follows:

Type:	flight_number	type_of_plane
	101	747
	205	737
	315	747
Gate:	flight_number	gate_number
	101	10
	205	15
	315	20

Then, for our interpretation, the set S is simply {<101,747>,<205,737>,<315,747>,<101,10>,<205,15>,1 <315,20>}. We have three function letters that we will denote by the names of the attributes in U, and two unary predicates that we will call Type and Gate. Thus Type(x) will mean that x is a variable that may be mapped to a tuple in the relation Type, and Gate(x) will mean that x is a variable that can be mapped to a tuple in the relation Gate.

Consider the simple alpha expression:

type_of_plane(x) : Type(x) AND E(y)((Gate(y) AND (flight number(x) = flight_number(y)) AND (gate_number(y) = a)))

It is easy to see that this expression corresponds to the set of queries: "Find the types of planes whose flights have gate number a." This is a set of queries rather than just one query because the interpretation of a has not been determined. As soon as we decide on the interpretation of the constant a, we have a query. For example, if the interpretation of a is 10, then the answer to the query is $\{<747>\}$. (We place $\{\ \}$ around 747 because the answer to a query is always a set of tuples—in this case a one-member set of one-tuples.

Once the constants in an alpha expression have been interpreted, the answer to a query is carried out by means of a generalization of the idea of satisfiability for the first-order logic. In the case of our query above, with a mapped to 10, we consider all pairs of tuples, t_1 and t_2, from the set S such that t_1 is a member of Type and t_2 is a member of Gate. We map x to t_1 and y to t_2. Having done that, Type(x) is satisfied by t_1, and Gate(y) is satisfied by t_2, and (gate_number(y) = 10) is satisfied only when t_2 = $<101,10>$, thus limiting us to pairs of tuples t_1 and t_2 where t_2 = $<101,10>$. Since there is only one tuple in Gate where flight_number = 101, namely t_1 = $<101,747>$, the only pair of tuples satisfying (flight_number(x) = flight_number(y)) AND (gate_number(y) = 10) is $<101,747>$ and $<101,10>$.

Finally, we select the members of $<101,747>$ and $<101,10>$ that are in our target list, in this case $\{<747>\}$. It is easy to check that the formulation of our alpha expressions depends only on the database scheme, and not on the relations that constitute an instance of the database scheme. Once the interpretation of the constants in the alpha expressions has been determined, the result of the query depends on the relations of the database scheme.

Codd defined a query language L to be relationally complete only if every query formulated by alpha expressions could be formulated in L. Date [26] outlines a proof that SQL is relationally complete.

11.11   Converting Alpha Expressions to SQL Expressions

Given the query

type_of_plane(x) : Type(x) AND E(y)((Gate(y) AND (flight number(x) = flight_number(y)) AND (gate_number(y) = 10)))

we can convert it to a SQL query as follows:

```
SELECT      type_of_plane
FROM        Type
WHERE       flight_number IN
(SELECT     flight_number
FROM        Gate
WHERE       gate_number = 10);
```

The following example illustrates the use of IMPLIES and a quantifier (y), and their translation to SQL.

type_of_plane(x) : Type(x) AND (y)((((Gate(y) AND (flight number(x) = flight_number(y)) AND (gate_number(y) = 10))) IMPLIES (type_of_plane(x) = 747))

Recall that A IMPLIES B is shorthand for NOT A OR B.

Consider the tuple <205,737> from Type. By rule 8 in Section 11.7 above, this tuple satisfies the qualification clause 5 if and only if every tuple t in Gate satisfies W = ((205 = flight_number(t)) AND (gate_number(t) = 10)) IMPLIES (737 = 747). Since no tuple in Gate SATISFIES ((205 = flight_number(t)) AND (gate_number(t) = 10)), every tuple in Gate SATISFIES W. Thus <205,737> SATISFIES the qualification clause of our query.

Furthermore, every tuple in Type satisfies our query. Thus, the result of our query is the list <747>, <737>.

Our query:

type_of_plane(x) : Type(x) AND (y)((((Gate(y) AND (flight number(x) = flight_number(y)) AND (gate_number(y) = 10))) IMPLIES (type_of_plane(x) = 747))

translates into SQL as

```
SELECT      type_of_plane
FROM        Type
WHERE       flight_number not IN
(SELECT     flight_number
FROM        Gate
WHERE       gate_number = 10)
OR          flight_number IN
(SELECT     flight_number
FROM        Gate
WHERE       (gate_number = 10) AND (type_of_plane = 747));
```

Other examples of translating tuple relational calculus expressions into SQL queries are given in the exercises at the end of this chapter.

Exercises

11.1. Express OR in terms of NOT and AND, and show that the resulting expression has the same truth table as OR.

11.2. Find an expression for exclusive OR in terms of NOT, AND, and OR; and compute the truth table to see that you have the correct expression.

11.3. Show that A IMPLIES A is a tautology.

11.4. a. Consider the following addition table for the integers mod(5). (Do ordinary addition. If the result is $>= 5$, repeatedly subtract 5 until the result is < 5.)

+	0	1	2	3	4
0	0	1	2	3	4
1	1	2	3	4	0
2	2	3	4	0	1
3	3	4	0	1	2
4	4	0	1	2	3

Make this into a model for the expression:

$$E = (x)((y)(E(z)(P(f(y,z),x)))).$$

b. Do the same for multiplication mod(5) and the expression:
$F = (x)((y)((\text{NOT } P(y,a)) \text{ IMPLIES } E(z)(P(f(y,z),x)))).$

c. Can we make multiplication mod(4) into a model for F?

11.5. Let T be the table below with attributes A, B, C such that, in a given row, the value in column A times the value in column B equals mod(3) the value in column C. Formulate a simple alpha expression to find the solution of the equation 2 times x = 1. Translate the alpha expression into a SQL SELECT query.

T

A	B	C
0	0	0
0	1	0
0	2	0
1	0	0
1	1	1
1	2	2
2	0	0
2	1	2
2	2	1

11.6. Consider the jail database with attribute set

U = {booking_number,
prisoner_name,
prisoner_alias,
prisoner_id_number,
date_of_birth,
date_of_arrest,
charge}.

Let the relation schemes for the jail database be
ID = {booking_number,prisoner_name,
    prisoner_id_number},
ALIAS = {prisoner_id_number,prisoner_alias},
BIRTH = {prisoner_id_number,date_of_birth},
ARREST = {booking_number,date_of_arrest,charge}.
Consequently, the database scheme is {ID,ALIAS,BIRTH, ARREST}.

For each of the following queries find an alpha expression and the corresponding SQL SELECT statement.
a. Find the names of all prisoners arrested on May 6.
b. Find all aliases of prisoners arrested May 6.
c. Find all the charges against the prisoner Donald Duck.
d. Find the names of all prisoners who were born on Sept 8, 1960.
e Find the names of all prisoners arrested May 6 charged with DUI.

Answers to Exercises

11.1. NOT((NOT A) AND (NOT B)). Compute the truth table in stages as follows:

```
NOT((NOT A    )    AND   (NOT B    ))

              TRUE                  TRUE

         FALSE                 FALSE
                         FALSE
    TRUE
NOT((NOT A    )    AND   (NOT B    ))

              TRUE                  FALSE

         FALSE                 TRUE
                         FALSE
```

TRUE

NOT((NOT A   )   AND (NOT B   ))

         FALSE   TRUE

    TRUE   FALSE

                  FALSE

TRUE

NOT((NOT A   )   AND (NOT B   ))

         FALSE   FALSE

    TRUE   TRUE

               TRUE

FALSE

11.2. (A OR B) AND (NOT(A AND B)). For A TRUE and B TRUE we have

(A   OR B   ) AND (NOT(A   ANDB   ))

TRUE   TRUE   TRUE   TRUE

    TRUE   TRUE

             FALSE

       FALSE

Check the other rows of the truth table similarly.

11.3. For A TRUE we have

    A   IMPLIES   A

  TRUE   TRUE

       TRUE

For A FALSE we have

    A   IMPLIES   A

  FALSE   FALSE

       TRUE

Since the bottom line is TRUE in both of the possible cases, we have a tautology.

11.4 a. Let f be mapped into addition as in the table. Let P be mapped into equality. Let S be the set $\{0,1,2,3,4\}$. Let SEQ be all two-element sequences of elements from S. For all members, $\{a,b\}$, of SEQ find a member c of S such that $b + c = a$. For example, $\{1,4\}$ is a member of SEQ, and we have $4 + 2 = 1$. Since it is possible to do this for every pair in SEQ, S, with the addition in the table, is a model for E.

11.4 b. In the case of multiplication mod(5) we have the table

x	0	1	2	3	4
0	0	0	0	0	0
1	0	1	2	3	4
2	0	2	4	1	3
3	0	3	1	4	2
4	0	4	3	2	1

Map a into 0, f into multiplication, and proceed as in the case of addition.

c. No. We have the table

x	0	1	2	3
0	0	0	0	0
1	0	1	2	3
2	0	2	0	2
3	0	3	2	1

and for the pair $\{1,2\}$ there is no a such that $a \times 2 = 1$.

11.5. The alpha expression is:
$t[B] : P_T(t)$ AND $((t[A] = 2)$ AND $(t[C] = 1))$.

A corresponding SQL expression is:

```
SELECT B
FROM T
WHERE A = 2 AND C = 1;
```

11.6. a. $t[\text{prisoner\_name}] :$
$ID(t)$

AND E(u)(ARREST(u)
AND (u(date_of_arrest) = May 6)
AND (u(booking_number) = t(booking_number)).

The corresponding SQL expression is

```
SELECT prisoner_name
FROM ID
WHERE booking_number IN
(SELECT booking_number
FROM ARREST
WHERE date_of_arrest = 'May 6');
```

b. t[prisoner_alias] :
ALIAS(t)
AND E(u)(ARREST(u)
AND (u(date_of_arrest) = May 6)
AND E(v)(ID(v)
AND (v(booking_number) = u(booking_number)
AND (v(prisoner_id_number) = t(prisoner_id_number)))))

The corresponding SQL expression is:

```
SELECT prisoner_alias
FROM ALIAS
WHERE prisoner_id_number IN
(SELECT prisoner_id_number
FROM ID
WHERE booking_number IN
(SELECT booking_number
FROM ARREST
WHERE date_of_arrest = 'May 6'));
```

c. t[charge] :

ARREST(t)
AND E(u)(ID(u)
AND (u(booking_number) = t(booking_number))
AND (u(prisoner_name) = Donald Duck))

The corresponding SQL expression is:

```
SELECT charge
FROM ARREST
```

```
WHERE booking__number IN
(SELECT booking__number
FROM ID
WHERE prisoner__name  =  ' Donald Duck');
```

d. *t*[prisoner__name] :

ID(*t*)
AND E(u)(BIRTH(u)
AND (T(prisoner__id__number) = u(prisoner__id__number))
AND (u(date__of__birth) = 'Sept 8 1960'))

The corresponding SQL expression is:

```
SELECT prisoner__name
FROM ID
WHERE prisoner__id__number IN
(SELECT prisoner__id__number
FROM BIRTH
WHERE date__of__birth  =  ' Sept 8 1960');
```

e. *t*[prisoner__name] :

ID(*t*)
AND E(u)(ARREST(u)
AND (t(booking__number) = u(booking__number))
AND (u(date__of__arrest) = May 6)
AND (u(charge) = DUI))

The corresponding SQL expression is:

```
SELECT prisoner__name
FROM ID
WHERE booking__number IN
(SELECT booking__number
FROM ARREST
WHERE date__of__arrest  =  ' May 6' AND charge  =  ' DUI');
```

12

Embedded SQL

THIS CHAPTER PRESENTS A VERSION OF SQL THAT CAN BE EMBEDDED in any programming language. This version will be useful for writing user programs to communicate with the database. We use the C programming language in our examples. For the reader who is not familiar with C, we recommend Kernighan and Ritchie[40].

Since most users have application tasks that have not been foreseen by the implementor, users must write computer programs to carry out these tasks. An example of such a task in our jail database (See Chapter 11, Exercise 6.) would be the job of sending information over a network about charges against a prisoner or list of prisoners. Since this task involves querying the database for each prisoner in the list, it is necessary to have a means of querying the database that can be built into the computer program.

Embedded SQL provides a means for building the necessary query into the computer program. Furthermore, embedded SQL makes it possible to write the program without knowing anything about the way in which the data are stored. In other words, embedded SQL maintains the ideals of relational databases and query languages such as SQL. By *ideals* we mean those stated by Codd [19,20] and others, which can be summed up as follows

- From the user's point of view, the database is a collection of tables, nothing more.

- All communication between the user and the database will take place through a query language or languages. By means of such a language, the user can tell what he wants, not how to get it.

The rest depends on the implementor. It is up to the implementor to provide the code to perform the commands of the query language.

In general the implementor will provide a precompiler to scan the code file for query language commands and replace them with host language code so that the program can then be compiled by a host compiler. It is up to the programmer to provide host language variables for the results of queries to be read into or for variable values in the query language conditionals. The latter are sometimes called *bind variables*. We shall adopt the term *bind* for such variables.

The implementor may also provide a library of modules to be called, with the query language commands passed to the modules. A library of modules has the following advantages:

- It is not necessary to use a precompiler. A precompiler frequently adds its own complications and is very time-consuming, especially during debug.

- It is in line with the way a programmer thinks—namely, in terms of calling modules to get certain things done.

- It is more flexible than a precompiler; that is, it does not impose any fixed structure on the source code.

- It is in line with the UNIX programming philosophy outlined in Kernighan and Pike[39]. We recommend that any programmer seeking to improve and simplify his programming technique read the philosophy in Kernighan and Pike.

The 1986 ANSI standard for SQL provides six pages of standards for embedded SQL, plus additional standards for embedding in COBOL, Fortran, Pascal, and PL/I. Standards for specific programming languages are superfluous since the precompiler will know what the host language is and need only be able to recognize the SQL statements—which should be the same for all host languages. In fact, standards for embedding in specific programming languages are worse than superfluous in that they embroil the programmer in many unnecessary details.

Instead, it should be required that the precompiler recognizes the embedded commands in any programming language in exactly the same way. Different precompilers should be required for different programming languages. Then, if you change programming languages, you don't need to learn a whole new set of details about embedded SQL. You only need to use a different precompiler.

12.1 Recognizing Embedded SQL Statements

All embedded SQL statements are preceded by the keywords EXEC SQL. Depending on the host programming language, they are terminated by a semicolon or some other terminator, or by no terminator at all. It would be very nice if the standards would select one terminator for all embedded SQL statements, for all host languages, for all time and thus eliminate the time wasted finding out what the terminator should be for a particular situation. Below, we shall assume that all embedded SQL statements are terminated by a semicolon.

12.2 A First Look at Embedded SQL

Given the initiator key words EXEC SQL and the semicolon terminator, many SQL statements can simply be embedded in the host language by writing them in, as for example:

```
EXEC SQL UPDATE ARREST
    SET charge = 'UID'
    WHERE prisoner_id_number = 111111;
```

or

```
EXEC SQL DELETE
    FROM ARREST
    WHERE prisoner_id_number = 111111;
```

12.3 Host Variables in Embedded SQL

Consider this SQL statement:

```
EXEC SQL SELECT charge
    FROM ARREST;
```

Where does charge go after it is selected? How does the program ever use it? What if there are multiple charges in ARREST? To answer these questions, SQL must be modified for embedding. Variables of the host programming language (COBOL, Fortran, the C language, or whichever it is) must appear in the embedded SQL statements.

Thus, one format for SELECT in embedded SQL is:

```
EXEC SQL SELECT <target list>
INTO <host variables>
FROM
WHERE
;
```

A specific example of this format is:

```
EXEC SQL SELECT charge
INTO :string
FROM ARREST
WHERE booking_number = :host_variable;
```

This format is acceptable if the query returns only one row. Otherwise, a work area is needed. In embedded SQL the work area is called a *cursor* (not to be confused with the flashing position marker on your screen). Cursors will be treated in Section 12.9 below.

In the last example, *string* and *host_variable* are host variables. In some implementations, every host variable in an embedded SQL expression is preceded by a colon (:) to differentiate it from a column name. We shall adopt this convention.

12.4   Variable Declaration

Those variables of the host language used in EXEC SQL statements must appear in a *declare section* in an appropriate place in the host program. *Appropriate* means that they have to be in an acceptable place after the precompiler finishes. For example, in the C programming language it is probably best to place them at the head of the file as externs.

The format is EXEC SQL BEGIN DECLARE to be followed by the variable declarations, which are followed by EXEC SQL END DECLARE.

12.5   SELECT in Embedded SQL

As shown above, the format for SELECT is:

```
EXEC SQL SELECT . . . INTO [list of host variables] FROM
      . . . WHERE . . .;
```

For example:

```
EXEC SQL SELECT prisoner__name INTO :string FROM ID WHERE booking__number
= 111111;
```

or

```
EXEC SQL SELECT prisoner__name INTO :string FROM ID WHERE booking__number
= :host__variable;
```

12.6 UPDATE in Embedded SQL

The format for UPDATE in embedded SQL is the same as the format for UPDATE given in Chapter 5 except that host variables may be used where appropriate. Here are some examples:

```
EXEC SQL UPDATE ID SET prisoner__name = 'John Smith'
WHERE booking__number = 111111;

EXEC SQL UPDATE ID SET prisoner__name = 'John Smith'
WHERE booking__number = :host__variable;

EXEC SQL UPDATE ID SET prisoner__name = :host__variable1
WHERE booking__number = :host__variable2;
```

12.7 DELETE and INSERT in Embedded SQL.

The format for DELETE in embedded SQL is the same as the format for DELETE given in Chapter 5 except that, as in the case of UPDATE, host variables may be used where appropriate. An example is:

```
EXEC SQL DELETE
   FROM ARREST
   WHERE charge = :host__variable;
```

Once again, the rules are the same as for INSERT in Chapter 5 except that host variables may be substituted where appropriate. For example

```
EXEC SQL INSERT
INTO ARREST (booking__number, charge)
VALUES (:host__variable1,:host__variable2);
```

12.8   Other Embedded SQL Commands

The rules for the COMMIT WORK, ROLLBACK WORK, and lock commands are exactly the same as they are when they are used outside of embedded SQL, except that they must be preceded by EXEC SQL and terminated by a semicolon (;).

12.9   Cursors

The result of a query is a virtual table or view. (It could turn out to be a base table as in the case of SELECT *.) The uses of such a table in an application program can be many and varied. A partial list is:

- Transfer it to hard copy. (Print it out.)

- Use it to make updates.

- Check integrity constraints.

- Move the information to a table somewhere else in a distributed database.

In any event, the results of a query frequently will contain many rows of multiple columns that will have to be dealt with one at a time in a program loop. Since most programming languages contain facilities for dealing with files, it is reasonable to treat the result of a query in a manner similar to a file that can be opened, read sequentially one row at a time, and closed when the end of file is reached.

The standard and practice have dictated that the entity corresponding to a file should be called a *cursor*. Why such a confusing name should have been chosen is a mystery buried in the past. The term as used here has nothing to do with the cursor on your screen. It is best to conceptualize it as a file somewhere. The specific implementation will determine where. The cursor must be associated with a query. The format for that is:

EXEC SQL DECLARE A CURSOR FOR [*SQL statement*];

The A in the above expression is variable and can be replaced by any name depending, of course, on any restrictions the implementor may have placed on the cursor name. (See your implementor's manual.) Think of A as being a symbol representing the work area where the outcome of your query will be placed (similar to a filename).

The SQL statement in the brackets can be either an actual SQL query or a string-pointer, host-variable name pointing to a string containing a SQL query statement (in which case it must appear in your EXEC SQL DECLARE section).

As discussed previously the semicolon on the end is a terminator. The ANSI standard states that the semicolon should be there if the host language is PL/I, but should not be there if the language is Fortran. It never mentions the C language. Perhaps there weren't any C programmers on the standards committee. This is one more example of the nightmare of details related to programming. In our view, the standard should say it is either there or not there, for all host languages, and for all time. Let the implementor of the precompiler worry about meeting the standard.

The best we can suggest is see your implementor's manual. To avoid having to make this statement over and over again, we can only suggest that, in each case, you read what's here and then check your implementor's manual; then pray that your implementor's manual is correct. If that fails, you can contact your implementor's customer support personnel.

The final alternative, of course, is to experiment. We suggest that all experiments should be done with very short, simple programs on very simple databases. Otherwise, you will probably end up being confused as to what the actual outcome of your experiment was.

Having given your cursor a name, you can open it. (Like a file). The format for this is

```
EXEC SQL OPEN A;
```

There is no reason why it should not be possible to have several cursors open at once. Of course, the implementation determines an upper limit on this.

To read your file-like cursor, there is the FETCH . . . INTO with format

```
EXEC SQL FETCH A INTO [list of host variable names]
```

(There is one host variable for each column name being selected.)

Presumably, the FETCH statement will be in some sort of loop in the host language whereby each row is dealt with in turn. Some implementations allow fetching into an array so that more than one row can be fetched at once. Fetching into arrays causes all kinds of complications. For one thing there is no way to know in advance how many rows are in the cursor. For example, if the cursor contains 42 rows and the arrays have 40 elements, two fetch operations will be required, and after the second fetch the program will have to check somehow for the number of rows returned. Since the fetch does not provide any way to obtain the number of rows returned, checking for the number of rows returned may require blanking one of the arrays and then checking for blanks after the fetch—which is a programming mess that may not work. Even if the fetch somehow returned information on the number of rows fetched, there is some added complication in using this information.

We suggest always fetching one row at a time, even if the implementation provides a way of finding out the number of rows fetched. All of the reasons we can think of for fetching more than one row at a time can be better provided for by modifying the query. For example, a sort can be provided for by including ORDER BY in the query. Some programmers think that they can get faster results by using FETCH for more than one row at a time and thereby avoiding multiple reads from the disk. This is not true if the implementation is properly designed. A properly designed implementation should have rapid I/O built in by means of buffering algorithms and the like.

When all of the fetches have been completed, it is a good idea to close the cursor in the same way you would close a file. The format for this is

```
EXEC SQL CLOSE A;
```

12.10   The SQLCODE Variable

How do you know if FETCH has fetched all the rows? How do you know if an error condition occurs in an EXEC SQL statement? The ANSI standard provides a variable SQLCODE and an *embedded exception declaration*, WHENEVER, with the conditionals SQLERROR and NOT FOUND, and the actions CONTINUE and GOTO <target>. At the target one can test the value of SQLCODE to find out what happened. ANSI leaves the specifics of SQLCODE up to the implementor.

We submit that WHENEVER is redundant, superfluous, and complicated, and that the enforced inclusion of GOTO is bad programming practice. It suffices to have the implementor provide an *include* file called SQLCODE (or whatever the implementor chooses to call it). One then places an include statement,

    include SQLCODE

at the head of the program file according to the syntax of the host language. The SQLCODE file provides the appropriate data structure(s) for the SQLCODE. The precompiler provides the code, placing the appropriate values and error messages in the data structures, which can be tested by the program after execution of the embedded statement, and if desired, the error messages can be output.

SQLCODE should be standardized to keep it simple. Perhaps one Boolean variable (TRUE or FALSE for error or not error), one integer variable (for error number), and one long string variable for error messages with some comments to aid the programmer would suffice. Some implementations provide such an include file.

In the following example, assume you want to send all the ARREST records of the prisoner whose prisoner_id is 111111 to someone over a network. Assume your host language is C, and that some of the suggestions above have been implemented; namely:

- WHENEVER has been eliminated.

- The header file SQLCODE exists and appears as follows:

```
struct sql_error {
    BOOLEAN sql_error_flag;    /* TRUE if error, FALSE otherwise */
    int error_number;   /* See error document */
    char error_message[150];
} SQLCODE;
BOOLEAN FETCH_not_finished;
/* Usually TRUE, FALSE if completed last FETCH */
```

Also assume that:

- We have a function error_handler( ) in some other file, which handles errors. It sends a message over the network that we have an error, does whatever is necessary to terminate the networking session, prints out the error_number and error_message, and exits.

- We have a function open_network( ) in some other file. It handles the necessary details to open the network for sending to whomever we want to send to. There exists a corresponding function close__network( ) in the other file.

• We have a function send( ) in some other file which sends the data over the network.

Our embedded SQL file might look like this:

```
#include "SQLCODE"
#define SIZE__OF__DATE X /* whatever the implementor size is for date */
#define SIZE__OF__CHARGE Y /* Y depends on CREATE TABLE ARREST */
int Bookno;
char Date[SIZE__OF__DATE];
char Charge[SIZE__OF__CHARGE];
char Sql1[ ] = "SELECT * FROM ARREST WHERE booking__number IN ";
char Sql2[ ] = "(SELECT booking__number FROM ID ";
char Sql3[ ] = "WHERE prisoner__id__number = 111111);";
char Sql[120];
main( )
{
    init( );
    EXEC SQL DECLARE A CURSOR FOR :Sql;
    if(SQLCODE.sql__error__flag)
      error__handler(&SQLCODE);
    EXEC SQL OPEN A;
    if(SQLCODE.sql__error__flag)
      error__handler(&SQLCODE);
    FETCH__not__finished = TRUE;
    while(FETCH__not__finished) {
      EXEC SQL FETCH A INTO :Bookno, :Date, :Charge;
      if(SQLCODE.sql__error__flag)
        error__handler(&SQLCODE);
      send(Bookno,Date,Charge);
    }
    close__network( );
    EXEC SQL CLOSE A;
    exit(0);
}
init( )
{
    strcpy(Sql,Sql1);
    strcat(Sql,Sql2);
```

```
        strcat(Sql,Sql3);
        open__network( );
    }
```

To slightly complicate this example, assume you have a list of 100 prisoner__id__numbers in a variable array in another file, and you want all charges for each. Then the code looks like this:

```
#include "SQLCODE"
#define SIZE__OF__DATE X /* whatever the implementor size is for date */
#define SIZE__OF__CHARGE Y /* Y depends on CREATE TABLE ARREST */
int Bookno,dummy;
char Date[SIZE__OF__DATE];
char Charge[SIZE__OF__CHARGE];
char Sql1[] = "SELECT * FROM ARREST WHERE booking__number IN ";
char Sql2[] = "(SELECT booking__number FROM ID ";
char Sql3[] = "WHERE prisoner__id__number = :dummy);";
char Sql[120];
extern int id__list[100];

main( )
{
int i;
    init( );
    EXEC SQL DECLARE A CURSOR FOR :Sql;
    if(SQLCODE.sql__error__flag)
        error__handler(&SQLCODE);
    for(i = 0;i < 100;i + +) {
        dummy = id__list[i];
        EXEC SQL OPEN A;
        if(SQLCODE.sql__error__flag)
            error__handler(&SQLCODE);
        FETCH__not__finished = TRUE;
        while(FETCH__not__finished) {
            EXEC SQL FETCH A INTO :Bookno, :Date, :Charge;
            if(SQLCODE.sql__error__flag)
                error__handler(&SQLCODE);
            send(dummy,Bookno,Date,Charge);
        }
        EXEC SQL CLOSE A;
    }
```

```
        close__network( );
        exit(0);
    }
```

If we use WHENEVER, main( ) can be shortened as follows:

```
    main( )
    {
    int i;
        init( );
        EXEC SQL WHENEVER SQLERROR GOTO error__point;
        EXEC SQL DECLARE A CURSOR FOR :Sql;
        for(i = 0;i < 100;i + +) {
            dummy = id__list[i];
            EXEC SQL OPEN A;
            FETCH__not__finished = TRUE;
            while(FETCH__not__finished) {
                EXEC SQL FETCH A INTO :Bookno, :Date, :Charge;
                send(dummy,Bookno,Date,Charge);
            }
            EXEC SQL CLOSE A;
        }
        close__network( );
        exit(0);
    error__point:
        error__handler( );
    }
```

WHENEVER would not be so obnoxious in C if it were not for the GOTO. Perhaps one day it will be modified to have a function call as follows:

```
EXEC SQL WHENEVER SQLERROR CALL error__handler(&SQLCODE);
```

The above example suggests what you need in the way of library functions for embedded SQL if you want to dispense with a precompiler. First, you would like to replace

```
EXEC SQL DECLARE A CURSOR FOR :Sql;
```

with a function declare( ), perhaps, with two arguments: the name of the cursor and a pointer to the SQL statement so that you could make a function call

```
declare("A",Sql);.
```

We would like declare( ) to allocate space for and return a pointer to a structure like the following

```
struct SQL__area {
    int Number__of__select__variables;
    struct Variable__data__area *Select__area;/* for FETCHed variables */
    int Number__of__bind__variables;
    struct Variable__data__area *Bind__area; /* for bind variables */
}
struct Variable__data__area {
    char *Column__name[ ];
    int *Column__size[ ];
    char *Column__type[ ];
    union data__types *types[ ];
}
union data__types {
    int integer__value;
    float float__value;

    char *string__value;
    Date date__value;          /* Date is a header file defined typedef */
    etc.                        /* depending on the implementation */

}
```

The struct Variable__data__area contains enough data for debugging purposes, as well as for almost any programming application.

For opening the cursor you need a function, SQL__open("A",SQL__area__pointer), perhaps, with two arguments, the name of the cursor and a pointer to a struct SQL__area. The reason SQL__open needs the SQL__area__pointer is that the values of the bind variables can be set in SQL__area__pointer->Bind__area->types before the SQL__open( ), thereby determining the result of the query.

For fetching you need a function

```
SQL__fetch("A",SQL__area__pointer)
```

with the same two arguments as open. SQL__fetch( ) fetches the current row of the cursor area into

SQL__area__pointer-> Select__area-> types

Similarly, for closing the cursor and freeing the space allocated for the SQL__area structure, you need a function, SQL__close("A",SQL__area__pointer), perhaps, with, again, the same two arguments. SQL__close( ) needs the SQL__area__pointer to free the space allocated for the SQL__area__pointer by declare( ).

Suppose you have the above described functions and a header file EMBED.H. If you assume that SQL__open( ), SQL__fetch( ), and SQL__close( ) return the SQLCODE.sql__error__flag, the code for our example above becomes

```
#include "SQLCODE"
#include "EMBED.H"
/* Notice you no longer need size of date or size of charge since they will be
returned in our SQL__area as will book__number, date, and charge */
char Sql1[] = "SELECT * FROM ARREST WHERE booking__number IN ";
char Sql2[] = "(SELECT booking__number FROM ID ";
char Sql3[] = "WHERE prisoner__id__number = :dummy);";
char Sql[120];
extern int id__list[100];
main( )
{
int i;
struct SQL__area *SQL__area__pointer;
    init( );
    SQL__area__pointer = declare("A",Sql);
    if(SQLCODE.sql__error__flag)
        error__handler(&SQLCODE);
    for(i = 0;i < 100;i + +) {
        SQL__area__pointer-> Bind__area-> types[0]-> integer__value
        = id__list[i];
        if(SQL__open("A",SQL__area__pointer))
            error__handler(&SQLCODE);
        FETCH__not__finished = TRUE;
        while(FETCH__not__finished) {
            if(SQL__fetch("A",SQL__area__pointer))
                error__handler(&SQLCODE);
            new__send(id__list[i],SQL__area__pointer);
        }
```

```
            if(SQL_close("A",SQL_area_pointer))
                error_handler(&SQLCODE);
    }
    close_network( );
    exit(0);
}
```

The advantages of the last sample code are the following:

- It is free of EXEC SQL lines and thus does not have to be precompiled.

- The data structure SQL_area_pointer contains all the information about the row last fetched that anyone could ever want.

    Thus, for example, you could replace new_send( ) by a function that would open another cursor based on the information in SQL_area_pointer.

- If your implementor does not supply the analogs of declare( ), SQL_open( ), SQL_fetch( ), and SQL_close( ), they can probably be written by the user using embedded SQL and utilities supplied by the implementor. Once written and debugged, the object modules can be stored in a library for use at link time.

12.11   The Use of Cursors for UPDATE and DELETE

Finally, we note that a cursor can be used to update or delete certain rows depending on tests of the value of those rows. The format for DECLARE in that case is:

```
EXEC SQL DECLARE A CURSOR FOR SELECT .......
    WHERE .........
    FOR UPDATE OF <column name>;
```

The point is that the rows in the cursor are ordered, either by an ORDER BY clause in the SELECT or by some other default value (See your implementor's manual). Then each FETCH moves the current position forward one row, and the UPDATE or DELETE can operate on the current row. After the cursor is closed, an EXEC SQL COMMIT WORK will commit the changes made in the cursor to the database.

The format for UPDATE to a cursor is:

```
EXEC SQL UPDATE <table name>
```

```
SET <column name>  =  <host__variable>
WHERE CURRENT OF A;
```

The column name above must be the same as the column name
in DECLARE above.

Similarly, the format for DELETE in a cursor is

```
EXEC SQL DELETE FROM <table name>
WHERE CURRENT OF A;
```

In summary, all SQL statements that do not involve arrays can
be embedded by preceding them with EXEC SQL and terminating
them with a semicolon. If arrays are involved, then cursors can be
used as in the above examples.

13

SQL at Work

A NUMBER OF COMMERCIAL DATABASES NOW INCORPORATE SQL AS THEIR data sublanguage. More are rumored to be on the way as the advantages of SQL become increasingly apparent to database professionals as well as to casual users.

After briefly discussing *System R*, which has served as a prototype of the relational database management system, this chapter will give an overview of some of the currently available commercial products now using SQL. These are *DB2*, *IMS*, *SQL/DS*, *ORACLE*, *Informix*, *SQLBASE*, *XDB*, and *Arity*. This list is necessarily incomplete—other systems using part or all of the SQL language are now on the market. Also, new relational systems are appearing each month, and new versions of previously nonrelational systems are now being offered in relational form, many using SQL. This is especially true in the microcomputer field. It would be impossible to list all such systems as they appear. Therefore, the following list is representative rather than exhaustive.

13.1 IBM *System R*

System R began as a research project designed to explore the possibilities and the practical utility of a relational database. The model had already been proposed by Codd *[14]*, but it remained to be shown that it could be successfully implemented and an efficient query language developed. A rich body of literature concerning practical considerations surrounding the relational database resulted from this effort. Much of this literature was cited in Chapter 1. Among the other spinoffs was the SQL query language.

The *System R* effort also developed the *User Friendly Interface* (UFI), a shared interface to the *System R* database, which accepts SQL expressions.

System R includes "embedded SQL," a modified form of SQL that can be used within a host programming language to facilitate the development of special-purpose applications.

Since *System R* was a research project rather than a commercial database, it was described in detail in the literature during its development, and therefore it has influenced a number of commercial databases that are now on the market.

13.2 The *Information Management System* (IMS)

IMS, The IBM *Information Management System* is an old and widely used database system running on large IBM 370 and 370-type machines using the MVS operating system. It is actually a hierarchical, rather than a relational system, but IMS data can be stored in a relational database and then queried, although not updated, by SQL.

13.3 The *SQL/Data System* (*SQL/DS*)

The *SQL/Data System* (*SQL/DS*), an IBM product, runs under either the IBM DOS/VSE or VM/SP operating system and is used on intermediate systems sized between mainframes and personal computers. *System R* preceded *SQL/DS* and therefore greatly influenced its design; however, there are differences: *SQL/DS* can extract data from IBM databases using the DL/1 query language of IMS. This feature allows data from a hierarchical database to be copied into a relational database and then queried using SQL.

SQL/DS uses an interactive SQL interface (ISQL) that is similar to *System R's* UFI and allows a user to enter SQL queries. ISQL also includes statements controlling the output format of query results, as well as commands to save and edit queries, and statements facilitating report generation.

13.4 *Database 2 (DB2)*

Database 2 (DB2), an IBM product, is used on large mainframes using the MVS operating system. Like *SQL/DS*, it has its origin in

System R. DB2 uses a Query Management facility (QMF) as the interface, allowing interaction between the database and SQL, as well as the Query By Example (QBE) language and a report writer facility. Since QBE is also a relational query language, DB2 offers its users both SQL and QBE.

DB2, introduced in 1983, has the capacity to handle large databases, and therefore is a relational competitor to the older, hierarchical IMS product.

13.5 *ORACLE*

ORACLE, a relational database management system available from Oracle Corporation, conforms closely to the user interface and query language of IBM's *SQL/DS*, especially in the early versions of *ORACLE*. The UFI of early versions has now been replaced with Oracle's own interface, *SQL*Plus*, in the most recent version. *ORACLE* runs on a wide variety of systems such as DEC VAX, and IBM 370-type computers, as well as on the AT&T 3B2 series and personal computers.

ORACLE also departs from similarity to the IBM systems in its report generation facility and in its concurrency control features.

ORACLE's *SQL*Report* is a multi table report generator; its *SQL*Forms* is a versatile forms-based application builder; and *SQL*Calc* offers spreadsheet convenience. *ORACLE* also has a line of "Pro" products for application development in high-level languages; programmers can then use precompilers to embed SQL statements in programs. These are: *Pro*C, Pro*COBOL, Pro*FORTRAN, Pro*PL/I, Pro*PASCAL,* and *Pro*ADA.*

Using an Ethernet LAN, network station PC's using *ORACLE* can be connected to a variety of powerful *ORACLE* database servers. Further details can be obtained from:

Oracle Corporation
20 Davis Drive
Belmont, CA 94002

13.6 *Informix*

Informix, a UNIX database system from Informix Software, Inc., runs on the IBM PC as well as many other computers and operating systems.

Informix Software, Inc. provides both *Informix/SQL* and a companion program *Informix 4GL*, which allows an application developer to use SQL in developing forms and reports.

Informix also provides two possibilities for local area networking (LAN), one PC-based running under MS-NET and the other a DOS-UNIX network that allows PC workstations to access an Informix database facility using UNIX.

Additional information can be obtained from

INFORMIX
4100 Bohannon Drive
Menlo Park, CA 94025

13.7 *SQLBASE*

The database management system *SQLBASE*, from Gupta Technology, runs under PC-DOS and is intended for the LAN market, although single-user systems are also available. *SQLBASE* centralizes record locking and recovery on the database server and therefore presents a unique package for LANs. *SQLBASE* can handle multiple requests from different workstations communicating with the central database server through SQL. It also can communicate with mainframe databases.

SQLBASE is equipped with a C language interface and will soon be available with a nonprocedural development tool called *Windows*, which is currently available only to C language programmers. More information can be obtained from

Gupta Technologies, Inc.
1040 Marsh Road, Suite 240
Menlo Park, CA 94025

13.8 *XDB*

The *XDB* database management system, available from Software Systems, Inc., uses SQL for *ad hoc* queries. It also provides a universal host-language interface so that programmers can access *XDB* databases by embedding SQL in COBOL, Pascal, or C language programs. As with most of the systems already discussed, *XDB* has an interactive report writer. Its form-development facility, however, has recently been enhanced, using SQL commands, to handle complex applications within an IF- THEN_ELSE structure. For more information, contact

Software Systems Technology
7100 Baltimore Ave., Suite 204,
College Park, MD 20740

13.9 *Ingress*

Ingres, one of the first commercial relational database management systems available, is also one of the few systems offering distributed processing as an option.

Ingres originally supported the structured query language called QUEL, but recently a SQL version has been added so that the user may choose which language (QUEL or SQL) to use.

Ingres now incorporates a full implementation of SQL, which includes a set of commands extending the SQL commands. The basic system includes a number of modules for querying by forms, generating reports, and executing interactive SQL commands. It can also be upgraded with an applications generator and embedded SQL.

Ingres is now available in a powerful PC version as well as for mainframes and minis. For more information about *Ingres*, contact

Relational Technology, Inc.
1080 Marina Village Parkway
Alameda, CA 94501

13.10 SQL as a Knowledge Base Query Language

A knowledge base is a database and a set of rules. As such, a knowledge base is used in the construction of an expert system, which emulates the reasoning of a human being in some field of knowledge.

In an expert system, exact answers to the queries posed to the knowledge base are not necessarily contained within the system, but the rules for obtaining an answer provide a means for arriving at a conclusion. The conclusion will not necessarily be an absolute answer with 100 percent certainty. Rather it should have about the same probability of being correct as would an expert in that field. This contrasts with a database where direct answers to queries are either contained within the system or are not there at all. Thus, we might refer to database systems as *query processors*, as Korth and Silberschatz [43] do, and to expert systems as *rule processors*, in which the answer sought is "data about data," i.e., "meta-data."

SQL can be used equally well with a database or a knowledge base, and several expert systems currently exist that use SQL.

Like databases, knowledge bases need to be updated from time to time, and additional data need to be inserted, as well as deleted. The SQL capabilities serve these purposes; however, knowledge bases have an additional problem in that rules that are added may contradict existing rules. Also, added rules may simply be extensions or necessary corollaries of existing rules, and therefore may be redundant. Testing for these problems quickly becomes onerous as the knowledge base grows large.

The expert system called *ARITY*, developed and sold by Arity Corporation, is an example of the use of SQL to access a knowledge base. For more information on the *ARITY* system, contact:

Arity Corporation
30 Domino Drive
Concord, MA 01742

Glossary

Glossary

aggregate function—A group function; a function operating on the values in one column of a table and producing a single value as its result.

alpha expression—Codd's term for a query in the tuple relational calculus.

argument—An expression inside the parentheses of a function, supplying a value for the function to operate on.

ASCII—A standard for using digital data to represent printable characters; an acronym for "American Standard Code for Information Exchange."

atomic formula—An n-place predicate with n terms filled in.

attribute—A column heading in a table.

base table—Any "real" table in the database, as opposed to a "virtual table."

Boolean operators—In relational algebra, Union (the set of all tuples that are in either one of two relations), Intersect (the set of all tuples that are in both of two relations), and Difference (the set of all tuples that are in one but not the other).

bound variable—An occurrence of a variable x in a wff X in which (x) or E(x) occurs in X, and the occurrence of x is within the scope of (x) or E(x); contrast with *free variable*.

C language—A programming language.

candidate row—A row selected by a main query, the field values of which are used in the execution of a correlated subquery.

cartesian product—An equijoin in which the set of conditions is empty.

category theory—A relatively new subject area of mathematics, developed in recent years as an approach to the foundations of mathematics, logic, interpretations, and models.

CHAR—A datatype that stores character strings.

character string—A sequence of characters.

COMMIT—To make permanent changes to the database. Before INSERTs, UPDATEs, and DELETEs are stored, both old and new data exist, so changes can be stored or data can be restored to its previous state. When data are COMMITted., all new data that is part of the transaction are made permanent, thereby replacing the old data in the database.

concatenated index—An index created on more than one column of a table, used to guarantee that those columns are unique for every row in the table.

database administrator (DBA)—A user authorized to grant and revoke other users' access to the system, modify options affecting all users, and perform other administrative functions.

Data Control Language (DCL)—One category of SQL statements; these statements control access to the data and to the database and include: GRANT CONNECT, GRANT SELECT, UPDATE ON, and REVOKE DBA.

Data Definition Language (DDL)—One category of SQL statements. These statements define (CREATE) or delete (DROP) database objects. Some examples are CREATE VIEW, CREATE TABLE, CREAT INDEX, and DROP TABLE.

data dictionary—A comprehensive set of tables and views usually owned by the DBA. Also contains information available to DBA only about users, privileges, and auditing. A central source of information for the database itself and for all users.

Data Manipulation Language (DML)—One category of SQL statements; these statements query and update the actual data. Examples include SELECT, INSERT, DELETE, and UPDATE.

datatype—Any one of the forms of data that are stored and manipulated. Major datatypes are: CHAR, DATE, LONG, NUMBER, and RAW.

date field—A field whose value is a date; sometimes applied to a field whose value is a number representing a date.

datum—A single unit of data.

DBA—See database administrator.

deadlock—A situation in which two users are each vying for resources locked by the other, and therefore neither user can obtain the necessary resource to complete the work.

default—The value of any option that is built into the system and will be used by the system if the user fails to specify a value for that option.

distinct—Unique.

domain relational calculus—One of the two forms of relational calculus in recent literature. (The other form is tuple relational calculus.) In domain relational calculus, the variables refer to attributes instead of rows.

dummy table—A table containing exactly one row and useful as the object of a SELECT command intended to copy the value of one field to another field.

embedded SQL—An application program consisting of programming language text and SQL text.

equijoin—A join condition specifying the relationship "equals" (=).

export—To transfer database files into some other storage area.

expression—One or more data items combined with operators or functions in a command.

field—A part of a table that holds one piece of data; the intersection of a row and a column.

filetype—The part of a file's name that describes the type of data stored in the file. Usually a file's filetype is separated from the filename by a period, as in, STORDATA.LIS, where LIS is the filetype.

foreign key—A column (or combination of columns) in one table that is not a key in that table but is a key elsewhere (e.g., in another table). Used for relating data in multiple tables using joins.

form feed—A control character that causes the printer to skip to the top of a new sheet of paper.

free variable—An occurrence of a variable x in X not within the scope of a quantifier (x) or E(x). Contrast with *bound variable*.

function—An operation that may be performed by placing the function's name in an expression. Most functions take one or more arguments within the parentheses and use the value(s) of the argument(s) in the operation.

group function—A function operating on a column or expression in all of the rows selected by a query, and computing a single value from them. Example: AVG, which computes an average. Also called aggregate function.

hexadecimal notation—A numbering system using base 16 instead of base 10. It represents the numbers 10 through 15 by the letters A through F. Often used to represent the internal (raw) values of data stored in a computer.

index—A feature used primarily to speed execution and impose uniqueness on data; provides faster access to data than doing a full table scan.

initialization—The initial preparing of a database, always done when installing a database system for the first time.

join—Retrieval from more than one table.

Julian date—A means of converting date data so every date can be expressed as a unique integer.

key—The column(s) in one table that can be used to uniquely identify a row. Column(s) forming a key are usually indexed.

main query—The outermost query in a query containing a subquery; the query that displays a result.

main variable—A variable that receives a field value in an EXEC SQL command.

modus ponens—A rule of inference whereby some wfs can be derived from others.

natural join—An equijoin taken on the common column of two tables with the duplicate of the common column removed.

nested SELECT—See *subquery*.

nesting—An arrangement of two processing steps in which one invokes the other.

non-equijoin—A join condition specifying a relationship other than "equals," e.g., <, >, < =, or > =.

null—Empty; not a value, but the absence of a value.

NUMBER datatype—A datatype for numeric data.

object—Something stored in a database. Examples: tables, views, synonyms, indexes, columns, reports, stored procedures, and stored programs.

outer join—The rows that do not match the join condition.

parameter—A column name, expression, or constant specifying what a command should do.

portability—The ease with which a computer program can be adapted to hardware different from that for which it was written.

precedence—The order in which the implementation performs operations on an expression.

precompiler—A program that reads a source program file and writes a modified source program file that a compiler can then read.

predicate clause—A clause based on one of the operators (= , ! = , IS, IS NOT, >, > =, <, < =) and containing no AND, OR, or NOT.

propagation—The process of copying a value from one field to another logically related field, or computing a value to be stored in a related field. For example, when an employee's social security number is entered in a block of a salary record form, it may be propagated to a block of a withholding tax form.

proof—A sequence of wfs such that each is either an axiom or can be derived from those preceding it by one of the rules of inference.

public synonym—A synonym for a database object that the DBA has created for use by all users.

query—An instruction to SQL that will retrieve information from one or more tables or views.

RAW datatype—Similar to CHAR datatypes, except that it stores uninterpreted bytes rather than characters.

read consistency—A feature whereby a SQL query always sees a snapshot of a table as it existed at the start of query execution even while others may be modifying the table.

record—One row of a table.

recursive definition—A definition in which the rule may be repeated an arbitrary number of times.

relational algebra—A set of operations on relations each of which produces other relations.

relational calculus—A development by Codd of the first-order logic for constructing queries on relational databases. It consists of the tuple relational calculus and domain relational calculus.

relational database—A database that appears to the user to be just a collection of tables.

reserved word—A word with a special meaning in SQL and therefore not available to users in naming tables, views, or columns.

ROLLBACK—Undo changes made to the database during a transaction or logical unit of work; opposite of COMMIT.

split-screen scrolling—A feature of some display devices making it possible to scroll data in a range of lines without affecting others parts of the screen.

SQL—See *Structured Query Language*.

Structured Query Language SQL—A basic user interface for storing and retrieving information in the database.

subquery—A query used as a clause in a SQL command.

substitution variable—A variable name or numeral used in a command file to represent a value that will be provided when the command file is run.

syntax—The linear order of words or symbols.

temporary tables—Tables frequently required to order data and to execute SQL statements, including the DISTINCT, ORDER BY, or GROUP BY clauses.

transaction—A logical unit of work as defined by the user.

transaction processing—The processing of logical units of work, rather than individual entries, to keep the database consistent.

truth function—A set of mappings from wfs to the set TF = (TRUE, FALSE). The main interpretation for the propositional calculus.

tuple—Row.

tuple relational calculus—One of the two types of the relational calculus. (The other is domain relational calculus.) In tuple relational calculus, the variables refer to tuples, or rows, in relations.

unique index—An index that imposes uniqueness on each value it indexes; may be a single column or concatenated columns.

union—The union operator of traditional set theory; for example, A UNION B (where A and B are sets) is the set of all objects x such that x is a member of A or x is a member of B, or both.

unit of work—A logical unit of work is equivalent to a transaction; includes all SQL statements since you either logged on, last committed, or last rolled back your work. A transaction can encompass one SQL statement or many SQL statements.

view—A table that does not physically exist as such in storage, but looks to the user as though it does. A part of a table that does exist in the database. A *virtual* table.

virtual column—A column in a query result, the value of which was calculated from the value(s) of other column(s).

virtual table—A table that does not actually exist in the database, but looks to the user as though it does. Contrast with *base table*. See *view*.

wff—A single well-formed formula.

wfs—More than one well-formed formula.

wrapping—Moving the end of a heading or field to a new line when it is too long to fit on one line.

References

1. American National Standards Institute. *American National Standard for information systems—database language—SQL. ANSI X3.135-1986.* New York: American National Standards Institute, Inc., 1986.

2. Astrahan, M.M., and Chamberlin, D.D. Implementation of a structured English query language. Comm. *ACM* 18, 10 (Oct. 1975): 580-588.

3. Astrahan, M.M.; Blasgen, M. W.; Chamberlin, D. D.; Eswaran, K. P.; Gray, J.N.; Griffiths, P. P.; King, W. F.; Lorie, R. A.; McJones, P. R.; Mehl, J. W.; Putzolu, G. R.; Traiger, I. L.; Wade, B.; and Watson, V. System R: A relational approach to database management. *ACM Transactions on Database Systems* (June 1976): 97.

4. Bancilhov, F., and Spyratos, N. Update semantics of relational views. *ACM Transactions on Database Systems* 6, 4 (Dec. 1981): 557-575.

5. Barr, M., and Wells, C. *Toposes, Triples and Theories* New York: Springer-Verlag, 1985.

6. Boyce, R. F., and Chamberlin, D. D. Using a structured English query language as a data definition facility. IBM Research Report RJ 1318 (#20559) December 10, 1973.

7. Boyce, R. F.; Chamberlin, D.D.; King, W. F.; and Hammer, M. M. Specifying queries as relational expressions: The SQUARE data sublanguage. *Comm. ACM* 18, 11 (Nov. 1975): 621-628.

8. Chamberlin, D. D., and Boyce, R. F. SEQUEL: A structured English query language. *Proc. ACM-SIGMOD Workshop on Data Description, Access, and Control, Ann Arbor, Mich.* (May 1974): 249-264.

9. Chamberlin, D. D.; Gray, J. N.; and Traiger, I. L. Views, authorization, and locking in a relational database system. *Proc. 1975 National Computer Conference Anaheim, Calif.*: 425-430.

10. Chamberlin, D. D.; Astrahan, M. M.; Eswaran, K. P.; Griffiths, P. P.; Lorie, R. A.; Mehl, J. W.; Reisner, P.; and Wade, B.W. SEQUEL 2: A unified approach to data definition, manipulation, and control. IBM J. Res. and Develop. 20, 6 (Nov. 1976): 560-575. (Also see errata in Jan. 1977 issue.)

11. Chamberlin, D. D. A summary of user experience with the SQL data sublanguage. *Proc. Internat. Conf. on Data Bases, Aberdeen, Scotland* (July 1980): 181-2-3. (Also see *IBM Res. Rep RJ2767*, San Jose, Calif.: April 1980).

12. Chamberlin, Donald D.; Astrahan, Morton M.; Blasgen, Michael W.; Gray, James N.; King, W. Frank; Lindsay, Bruce G.; Lorie, Raymond; Mehl, James W.; Price, Thomas G.; Putzolu, Franco; Selinger, Patricia Griffiths; Schkolnick, Mario; Slutz, Donald R.; Traiger, Irving L.; Wade, Bradford W.; and Yost, Robert A. A History and Evaluation of System R. *Communications of the ACM* 24, 10, (Oct. 1981).

13. Church, Alonzo. *Introduction to Mathematical Logic*, Princeton, N.J.: Princeton University Press, 1956.

14. Codd, E. F. A relational model of data for large shared data banks. *Comm. ACM* 13, 6 (June 1970): 377-387.

15. Codd, E. F. Normalized data base structure: A brief tutorial. *Proceedings of the 1971 SIGFIDET Workshop, Data Description, Access, and Control*, Ed. E. F. Codd and A. L. Dean.

16. Codd, E. F. A data base sublanguage founded on the relational

calculus. *Proceedings of the 1971 ACM SIGFIDET Workshop, Data Description, Access, and Control*. Ed. E. F. Codd and A. L. Dean.

17. Codd, E. F. "Relational Completeness of Data Base Sublanguages." In *Data Base Systems*, Courant Computer Science Symposia Series, Vol. 6, Englewood Cliffs, N. J.: Prentice-Hall, 1971.

18. Codd, E. F. "Further Normalization of the Data Base Relational Model." In *Data Base Systems*, Courant Computer Science Symposia Series, Vol. 6. Englewood Cliffs, N.J.: Prentice-Hall, 1971.

19. Codd, E. F. "Is Your DBMS Really Relational?" *Computerworld*, Oct. 14, 1985.

20. Codd, E.F. "Does Your DBMS Run by the Rules?" *Computerworld*, Oct. 21, 1985.

21. Codd, E.F. Extending the relational model to capture more meaning. *ACM Transactions on Database Systems* (Dec. 1979): 397-434.

22. Cohn, P. M. "Relational Structures and Models." In *Universal Algebra*, New York: Harper & Row, 1965.D06

23. Cosmadakis, S., and Papadimitriou, C. H. Updates of relational views. *Proc. 2nd ACM SIGACT-AIGMOD Symposium on Principles of Database Systems* (March 1983).

24. Dahl, Veronica. On database systems development through logic. *ACM Transactions on Database Systems 7*, 1 (March 1982.

25. Date, C. J. *A Guide to DB2*. Menlo Park, Calif.: Addison Wesley, 1985.

26. Date, C. J. *An Introduction to Database Systems*, Vol. 1, 4th Edition. Menlo Park, Calif.: Addison Wesley, 1986.

27. Date, C. J. *Relational Database: Selected Writings*. Menlo Park, Calif.: Addison Wesley, 1986.

28. Date, C. J. An architecture for high-level language database extensions. *Proc. ACM SIGMOD Conference* (June 1976): 101.

29. Dayal, U., and Bernstein, P.A. On the correct translation of update operations on relational views. *ACM TODS 7 3* (Sept. 1982).

30. Fagin, R.; Ullman, J. D.; and Vardi, M. Y. On the semantics of updates in databases. *Proc. 2nd ACM SIGACT-SIGMOD Symposium on Principles of Database Systems (March 1983).*

31. Finkelstein, Richard. "How to Choose SQL Database Management System." Data Base Advisor 5, 4 (April 1987).

32. Furtado, A. L., and Casanova, M.A. "Updating Relational Views." In *Query Processing in Database Systems* (eds. W. Kim, D. Reiner, and D. Batory). New York: Springer-Verlag, 1985.

33. Goguen, J.A. and Burstall, R. M. "Introducing Institutions, Lecture Notes." In *Logics of Programs* Workshop. Carnegie Mellon Univ., Pittsburgh, Pa. Computer Science 164, June 6-8, 1983. Berlin: Springer-Verlag, 1984.

34. Hursch, J. L., and Hursch, C. J. *Working With ORACLE: An Introduction to Database Management.* Blue Ridge Summit, Pa.: TAB BOOKS Inc., 1987.

35. IBM DATABASE 2 *Introduction to SQL.* GC26-4082, 1986. SC26-4082-2.

36. IBM DATABASE 2 *Data Base Planning and Administration Guide.* SC26-4077.

37. IBM DATABASE 2 *Sample Application Guide.* SC26-4086.

38. Keller, A. M. "Updates to Relational Databases through Views Involving Joins." In *Improving Database Usability and Responsiveness* (ed. P. Scheuermann). New York: Academic Press, 1982.

39. Kernighan, B. W., and Pike, R. *The Unix Programming Environment.* Englewood Cliffs, N.J.: Prentice-Hall, 1984.

40. Kernighan, B. W., and Ritchie, D. M. *The C Programming Language.* Englewood Cliffs, N.J.: Prentice-Hall, 1978.

41. Kim, Won. On optimizing an SQL-like nested query. *ACM Transactions on Database Systems 7, 3 (Sept. 1982): 443-469.*

42. Kim, W.; Reiner, D.; and Batory, D. (eds.) Query

Processing in Database Systems. New York: Springer-Verlag, 1985.

43. Korth, Henry F., and Silberschatz, Abraham. *Database System Concepts.* New York: McGraw-Hill, 1986.

44. Lewis, H. R., and Papadimitrious, C. H., *Elements of the Theory of Computation.* Englewood Cliffs, N.J.: Prentice-Hall, 1981.

45. Lipski, W., Jr., On semantic issues connected with incomplete information databases. *ACM TODS* 4 3 (Sept. 1979).

46. Maier, David. *The Theory of Relational Databases,* Rockville, Md.: Computer Science Press, 1983.

47. Makkai, Michael, and Reyes, Gonzalo E. "First Order Categorical Logic." In *Lecture Notes in Mathematics.* A. Dold and B. Eckmann (Eds.) New York: Springer-Verlag, 1977.

48. Marcus, Claudia. *Prolog Programming.* Menlo Park, Calif.: Addison-Wesley, 1986.

49. Mendelson, Elliott. *Mathematical Logic.* Princeton, N.J.: D. Van Nostrand Company, Inc., 1964.

50. Nauer, P. Report on the algorithmic language ALGOL 60*. *Communications of the ACM* 6,1 (1963): 1-17.

51. Oracle Corporation. *SQL*Plus User's Guide.* Belmont, Calif.: Oracle Corporation, 1986.

52. Tarski, A. *Logic, Semantics, Metamathematics.* Oxford Univ. Press, 1956.

53. Ullman, Jeffrey D.. Implementation of logical query languages for databases. *ACM Transactions on Database Systems* 19, 3 (Sept. 1985): 289-321.

54. Welty, Charles, and Stemple, David W.. Human factors comparison of a procedural and a nonprocedural query language. *ACM Transactions on Database Systems* 6, 4 (Dec. 1981): 626-649.

55. Yang, Chao-Chih. *Relational Databases.* Englewood Cliffs, N.J.: Prentice-Hall, 1986.

Index

Index

Edited by Stephen Moore

Other Bestsellers of Related Interest

SUPERCHARGED GRAPHICS: A Programmer's Source Code Toolbox—Lee Adams

This advanced graphics learning resource provides programs from which you can create your own graphics. Complete source code and user documentation are given for four major programs: drafting, paintbrush, 3D CAD, and animation. Covering hardware, software, and graphic management aspects, this computer-graphics tutorial demonstrates keyboard control techniques, mouse control techniques, and more! 496 pages, 180 illustrations. Book No. 2959, $19.95 paperback, $29.95 hardcover

THE C TRILOGY: A COMPLETE LIBRARY FOR C PROGRAMMERS—Eric P. Bloom

Far more than just another programming tutorial or collection of subroutines and functions, this is a complete single-volume C reference library. It gives you access to information you need to learn the C language and to write and use C programs on your IBM PC or compatible microcomputer. There's even a toolbox collection of 196b ready-to-use subroutines and functions that are guaranteed to save you time and effort. 510 pages, 211 illustrations. Book No. 2890, $22.95 paperback, $34.95 hardcover

---

Look for These and Other TAB Books at Your Local BOOKSTORE

To Order Call Toll Free 1-800-822-8158
(in PA and AK call 717-794-2191)

or write to TAB BOOKS Inc., Blue Ridge Summit, PA 17294-0840.

Title	Product No.	Quantity	Price

☐ Check or money order made payable to TAB BOOKS Inc.

Charge my ☐ VISA ☐ MasterCard ☐ American Express

Acct. No. _____ Exp. _____

Signature: _____

Name: _____

City: _____

State: _____ Zip: _____

Subtotal $ _____

Postage and Handling ($3.00 in U.S., $5.00 outside U.S.) $ _____

In PA, NY, & ME add applicable sales tax $ _____

TOTAL $ _____

TAB BOOKS catalog free with purchase; otherwise send $1.00 in check or money order and receive $1.00 credit on your next purchase.

Orders outside U.S. must pay with international money order in U.S. dollars.

TAB Guarantee: If for any reason you are not satisfied with the book(s) you order, simply return it (them) within 15 days and receive a full refund.
BC